A

MENTAL TOOTH-PICK

FOR

THE FAIR SEX;

OR,

SOMETHING USEFUL *to occupy their* TIME, *in the*
Abfence of BETTER AMUSEMENT.

La prudence vous conduit a une vie aifee et tranquille,
que tous les emplois bruyans ou autres accompliffemens
ne peuvent nous donner.

Prudence conducts us through life with that eafe
and tranquillity, which all the boafted offices of
other accomplifhments can never confer.

EDINBURGH:
PRINTED BY SCHAW AND PILLANS
And fold by J. GUTHRIE, Nicholfon's Street, and
W. DICKSON, High Street, Edinburgh.

1797.

TO

CLEMENTINA GOODALL.

W HAT a pity that fo handfome a name fhould be fo often and fo much abufed ! It is fome fmall confolation, however, that the feafon is faft approaching, when in reality it will be faluted with proper refpect. We are affured, that in the realms of never-ending day, neither a counterfeit nor bafe metal, though ever fo nicely gilded, fhall pafs for current coin. And it were to be wifhed, that, even in the prefent ftate, the diftinction was fomewhat more minutely obferved. Clementina, my addrefs to thee fhall not

confift

confift in flówers of learning, polifhed periods, or
nicely ftudied compliments ; a few plain truths,
expreffed in fimple language, is all thou haft to
expect : and if this mode fhould happen to hit
thy tafte, fo much the better for me. It is true,
in many dedications it is ufual to rifle the apartments of the dead, and bring back a long lift of
anceftors, with their wonderful atchievements ;
ornamented with all the ftudied decorations of
highly exaggerated praife; but as I am not fo well
acquainted with your relations, as would be neceffary for a juft delineation of their refpective
characters, fuch an omiffion will require no apology. I am forry to fay, that even my intimacy
with yourfelf was too much in the *en paffant*
ftyle : therefore my whole panegyric fhall confift of this fingle obfervation, that you appeared
modeft, comely, and well-made. If this account
fhould chance to meet your eye, and you fhould
be able to know yourfelf, and find from this

mode

mode of addrefs who I am, I fhall furely refpect your ingenuity, and allow you more than
ordinary penetration. If Fate, as I fincerely
wifh it may, fhould confent to our better acquaintance, and that I' find your other accomplifhments correfpond to your external appearance, I fhall be more liberal in my future encomiums ; and till that is the cafe, I hope you
will excufe me for being fo referved. Adieu,

Dear Clementina,

And believe me to be yours with the

fincereft refpect and efteem,

Candid-hall, }
May 1797. } PHILOGUNA.

N.B. It was faid of a painter, not very re-
markable in his profeffion, that upon fhewing
the great Apelles a picture of his, and inform-
ing him at the fame time, that he had taken but
a few hours to finifh it, he received this reply,
" Though you had not told me fo, yet I plainly

A 3   fee

fee caufe enough to believe, that it is no more than a hafty draught." An apology, or expreſſions ſimilar to this obfervation, was juſt what I once intended ; but I have now thought of changing this cant, and, inſtead of telling the world that it is the hafty production of a few days, I think it is better to be modeſt, and fay nothing about the time I employed in preparing it, leſt I ſhould only betray my ignorance and felf-conceit ; acquaintances with which I may be familiar enough, though I ſhould not publiſh it to the world, by fuch faſhionable excuſes. It would feem, from my being fo very fond of my own invention, that I really thought others would be equally fo ; and that it would be a great difappointment to the impatient crowd, who were eagerly gaping to fwallow my wonderful performance, if they were not as rapidly favoured with it, as I had been in preparing it. But thefe ideas in reality I do not entertain. I am perfectly convinced,

vinced, that the world would not mifs either myfelf or my child; but if the judicious part of
mankind will fuffer this production to pafs un-
molefted, I fhall thank them for their kindnefs.
I care not from what motive the indulgence proceeds, whether from compaffion or approbation;
though I muft confefs, that the latter is what I
fhould wifh to merit. I know full well, that the
Public is not to be much interefted in the fate
of my Pick, but it concerns me to make fuch
conceffions as are confiftent with plain honefty.
Original colouring is the principal feature of
this performance. Some thoughts, I acknowledge, are borrowed, and manufactured in my
own ftyle; fuch paffages as I thought related to
my fubject, I have liberally quoted. But even
after this confeffion, I by no means confider it
as a fpurious progeny, If any perfon fhould
fay otherwife, however, and claim it as his own
property, I fhall not think it worth while to
                                        quarrel

quarrel with him, fend him a challenge, nor even
trouble him with much contradiction.

MENTAL

MENTAL TOOTH-PICK.

Great bleffings ever wait on virtuous deeds,
And though a late, a fure reward fucceeds.

CONGREVE.

I have always been of opinion, that witticifm in poffeffion of an ill-natured or imprudent perfon is a dangerous weapon. Though ever fo innocent, it fhould be cautioufly employed. A fatirift and lampooner, who are in their element only when their captious humour inflames as it operates, are neither proper fubjects of panegyric, nor fit copies for imitation.—Therefore my Pick fhall fmell but little of their oil.

It is not neceffary to import the materials of my fimple inftrument from foreign lands; nor are the mines of Peru the proper place to find them; they lie within the reach of all who figh

for

for an acquaintance with virtue, of all who revere her venerable form ; for in mental reflection the fearch is gratified, and the fecret difcovered. I have ferved an apprenticefhip under
the influence of the torrid zone, and know the
fuperiority of an accomplifhed female too well,
ever to difrefpeft that valuable charafter. I
fhould not in the leaft quarrel with any fenfible
writer, for inverting the propofition of a great
moralift in the following manner : A candid virtuous female is the nobleft work of God, and
the brighteft part of the creation.

From this plain declaration, the female of reputation may eafily perceive, fhe has nothing to
dread from the pen of one who ever has, and
ftill continues to wear, the livery of fincere af-
feftion. If the caufe of female merit fhould receive no great luftre from fo weak an advocate,
that of innocence fhall never fuffer any falfe con-
ftruftion, or ungenerous reprefentation, from any
feeble effort of mine.

Having proceeded thus far in the ftyle of ego-
tifm, which an eminent charafter, who was
well acquainted with the rules of politenefs, and
knew equally well how to defcribe the effentials

of

of good breeding, fo much and ftrongly difcom-
mends, I fhall take an opportunity of entering
into a more eligible direction, as foon as I can
get rid of a necefſary prelude, which requires
fome little inveftigation.

Some may apprehend, that a tooth-pick is a
piece of furniture that can eafily be wanted ; and
that many ufe it more by way of ornament, than
as an inſtrument necefſary for removing pain,
or promoting pleaſure. Small as it is, however, unleſs ingeniouſly managed, it may commit leſs or more miſchief; it may wound the
tongue, and give a cloudy colour to the gums. But
if, upon reflection, its good qualities are found to
overbalance any inconvenience or bad effects
that may attend its uſe, it would be improper to
lay it aſide, and noways criminal to employ fo
fmall a piece of luxury. Crumbs of food, lying
in a ftate of putrefaction, are of a corroſive nature, and in a fhort time may hurt the enamel
of the teeth. Removing this preffure is of great
advantage, as it helps to keep them clean, and to
preferve their poliſh ; and a cafe of beautiful
teeth is no fmall ornament, to either male or female : if, then, it is found fo necefſary for the
body,

body, why may not one be invented for the mind?
and as I suppose mine is the first that has been
made of the mental kind, I hope, if females of
character (the only part of the sex whose good
opinion I am desirous to obtain) do not think me
deserving of a premium, they will at least approve of my Pick, for the novelty of the phrase.
In every well regulated society, where the periods of civilization extend their graceful progrefs, the mechanical labour of the artist, in
every new invention, where any degree of ingenuity is displayed, calls for the eye of public inspection, to examine its value, construction, and
symmetry; and praise is annexed to the performance, corresponding in some measure to the inven-
tor's merit. A patent, to perpetuate his memory,
is granted by public authority; he receives a
generous reward, accompanied with sonorous
peals of applause. Have I any claim to such expectations or privileges? Alas! my flattering
career has now lost its wheels, and my soaring
hope is deprived of its wings; for all I have to
boast of, is no more than coining a new epithet
for reflection. If my sincerity, and the honesty
of my intention, fail to procure me the good-
will

will of mankind, I doubt much of meeting it in the way of merit.

An eminent writer juftly obferves, with his ufual flowers of elegance, " That the acknow-ledgement of thofe virtues on which confcience congratulates us, is a tribute that we can at any time exact with confidence; but the celebration of thofe virtues we only feign or defire, without any vigorous endeavours to attain them, is received as a triumph over regions, not yet conquered."—Delightful fcenes pleafe a correct tafte, and the benefit of information will always excite the induf-try of thofe who fearch for refinement.

The female who is familiar with labours of merit, who longs to learn what is beautiful in the production of arts, as well as what is inge-nious in the delineation of morals, will not in the leaft be offended to meet here with a beautiful quotation from a mafterly pencil, on the fubject of education : " Should a mafter, after having given his pupil a few lectures on the elements of grammar, leave him at liberty to make the beft of his way through the claffes, without giving him the leaft affiftance in the progrefs of his ftudies,

or

or pointing out the use and application of the necessary rules as he advanced in his learning, is it to be thought from this superficial instruction he would be found a complete scholar? Common sense will at once make the proper reply; and shall less pains or care be thought sufficient to nurse the virtues of the heart? to form him a good man, or a valuable member of the community to which he belongs? Is it easier, after having learned the rudiments of knowledge and morality, for a character to guide himself with nice taste, or correct judgement, in the labyrinth of life, and steer unshaken, in full triumph, a steady course of virtue, through the shoals, rocks, and all the other dangers he has to encounter, in a vessel without ballast, ignorant of her motion, and the skill required in her management, to subdue the swelling tide of corruption, and the boisterous storms of passion, than to understand the sense of a Roman or a Greek author?" When Ulysses intrusted the education of his son to the nobles of Ithaca, to one of them, in particular, he enforces the charge with this affectionate address, " O my friend, if ever you loved his father, shew him some proof of it in your care of his son, but

above

above all do not omit to form him juft, fincere, and faithful."

The beft method (fays Socrates to his pupil Alcibiades) that you can make ufe of to draw the bleffings of heaven upon yourfelf, and to render your prayers acceptable, will be found connected with the conftant practice of your duty towards God and men. From thefe examples, we plainly fee the anxiety which prevailed, in the former ages of the world, for improving the youthful mind. It would be a pity, if the prefent race and æra, fo far advanced in refinement, fhould in any point or fcience have caufe to blufh at a comparifon with ancient days. When a painter examines a new picture, he not only attends to the brightnefs of the colours, but the delicacy of the connected parts, and the art by which the whole is conducted. It is the nice junction or uniformity of the concordant lines, that principally excite notice, and furnifh matter for approbation. Though I cannot promife my reader a model of finifhed arrangement, or elegance of conception, ftill a defire to trace the pure fprings of truth, reafon, and religion, I

B 2   flatter

flatter myfelf, will apologife for my defects, and
procure me fome little indulgence.

Refinement of mind, in every age and country,
has been always thought the principal part of
beauty. If education is admitted to be an effectual mean of attaining this rich ornament, then
it is a felf-evident truth, that it can never be too
ftrongly recommended, nor too clofely cultivated.
Is the contemplation of female elegance, where-
ever it is feen, an object of delight? Is not the
tribute of refpect, and the partiality paid to it,
when it appears to advantage, a powerful motive for encouraging a fpirit of improvement?
Let us paufe a little, and look around us, let us
fee how much birth itfelf is adorned by a regular education; how a genteel female, by the careful labour of a 'few years, rifes to notice and
refpect, and ftands poffeffed of ornaments that
will remain in honour till the lateft period of life;
ornaments which have the initials of knowledge,
goodnefs of heart, and genuine religion, ftrongly
imprefled on their front; though they fhould not
be altogether the tone of the times, nor particularly in vogue, the improvement of fuch lafting
ornaments cannot fail, in the courfe of years, to

reflect

reflect luftre and credit on the wife female who
has judgement fufficient to difcern their value,
and fteadinefs enough to perfevere in their purfuit. A conftant and juft fenfe of decorum in
every opening fcene, imparts the pureft emotions of
pleafure. How refined are her enjoyments, whofe
tafte is regulated by the dictates of a well-informed
mind. The eye of penetration muft admire the
female who is capable of being charmed, and of
charming in her turn. The advantages of birth
or fortune may fecure the adoration of the vulgar ; but fhe who excels in mental refinement,
courteous behaviour, and an agreeable temper,
fhows the effentials of a correct and delicate
beauty ;—ornaments which command the refpect
of fuperior tafte, of thofe who more highly admire the merit of a ripe underftanding, than the
accidental advantages of external form. The
charms of novelty, like the unfettled bloffoms of
fpring, wear a dazzling appearance, but are
eafily defaced ; and when once they fade can never be renewed. The flighty character, like a
temporary ballad, is only in requeft for a little
while ; but a modeft fenfible female will long
continue to fupport her character. Curiofity is

awakened

awakened at the firft fight of an elegant dome, but it is the riches within that eftablifhes its lafting fame. The merit of a female is not altogether to be eftimated from her great qualities, it is the placing them in a proper attitude that fhows them advantageoufly. A foil, though originally fertile, if left without culture, will foon contract barrennefs, and wear the face of a lonely defert; whereas a piece of land naturally fterile, and of a furface feemingly crowded with inequalities, by the ingenious hand of induftry, may be made in a fhort time, not only to compenfate the cultivator's toil, but even to vie with the firft-rate productions of nature. The Grecians improved the arts and fciences to fuch a height, that the claim of competition was every where relinquifhed, and the laurels of knowledge flourifhed at Athens, with a degree of verdure which at that time appeared to furpafs the reft of the world. Neighbouring nations admired their genius, and confidered them as finifhed and inftructive examples for their careful imitation.

If writers defcribe the Turks as fomewhat flow or phlegmatic in mental proficiency, they take care to fupply that deficiency by cloathing

them

them with beauties no lefs engaging : they fpeak
of their morals as gracefully polifhed, and almoft irreproachable : for moderation of their
paffions, and fidelity to their word, they are allowed to be peculiarly diftinguifhed. The Romans, early in life, acquired a tafte peculiar to
themfelves. Female education was confidered as
a matter of the utmoft importance. Matrons of
eftablifhed reputation were looked upon with refpect, and as mothers to whom the facred pledges
of affection, diftinguifhed either by character or
family, might be fafely intrufted. What a
pleafant tafk to guide the tender mind with
prudence and fafety, over the falfe and dangerous rocks that lie concealed in the fea of
life, and of which the thoughtlefs inexperience
of youth could have no juft conception. Who
then fo fit for this important duty, as a virtuous
female, rendered venerable by age, and diftinguifhed by folidity of judgement, who poffeffes an extenfive ftock of knowledge, and is
univerfally refpected as the honour of her fex.
Judicious fentiments, expreffed in plain language,
unfophifticated reafoning on intellectual accomplifhments, and daily leffons on moral purity, as
the

the greateft ornament of the fex, would found
from the lips of fuch a character, with a ftrain
of the powerfulleft eloquence : and when a fair
copy of the inftructions fhe inculcated was ex-
preffively reprefented in her own conduct, they
could fcarcely fail to be irrefiftibly impreffive.

" In articles of tafte and luxury," as obferved
by a very learned writer, " the demand appears
fo arbitrary, as fcarce to be reducible to any eftablifhed rules." Notwithftanding of this affertion, the figures and numbers which compofe
the character of beauty, may in fome meafure
be difcovered without the art of logic. In my
opinion, it is not neceffary to ranfack the field of
literature for information on the point; it furely
confifts in the harmony of the heart, and the fabric is formed by the continued union of the
richeft materials. A natural honefty of look,
fupported by confcioufnefs of rectitude, triumphs over all artificial beauty. Regular features, brightened by goodnefs of heart, and mildnefs of difpofition, like the fhades in painting,
give relief to neighbouring virtues, and make
the whole figure altogether lovely. Tafte, rou-
fed by emulation, refines gradually; and from a

careful

careful imitation of beauties, the mind imperceptibly advances towards its higheſt improvement. But where no ſuperior model appears to be conſulted, or to excite laudable ambition, the field of refinement muſt be barren indeed. Though I thought to have made a new diſcovery that had eſcaped the notice of the learned, I find myſelf ſo much entangled, that I muſt relinquiſh my own fanciful excurſion, and coincide with information more ripe than my own. It is true, if we conſult the collected treaſures of the hiſtorian, or peruſe the laboured periods of the poet, we ſhall find their delineation of characters commonly drawn from the flowers of the heart, or the rich colours of virtue. But if we look around us, and examine human nature with any degree of attention, we ſhall find, that the moſt of mankind judge of beauty agreeably to their own fancy or caprice; ſome, from the wild conceits of a vitiated imagination, and others from reaſon and a correct taſte. If the opinion of my landlady is aſked, I think her ſentiments will be much in this ſtyle: " She that has feweſt faults, and acts beſt." The affable modeſt look, the benevolence which tenderly

breathes

breathes in every expreffion, and foftly fmiles in
every duty; thefe, in her book of calculation, are
firft-rate ornaments: Thefe will endure the
fummer heat, and winter's cold, and will not fall
like leaves in autumn. Such genuine marks of
diftinction will always continue engaging, and
fhe who is in poffeffion of fo much grace will
find her jubilee return with every rifing fun;
for the outward endowments of nature, or the
higheft improvements of art, when compared
with the goodnefs of the heart, are low and artificial. This idea of beauty is very neceffary to
be encouraged at all times, particularly in early
life, not only becaufe the moft important, but
the firft impreffions are moft likely to continue,
efpecially when the underftanding afterwards
finds fufficient reafon to juftify its early partiality. When, with the dawning of the day, every
elegant accomplifhment is carefully nurfed, and
the mind by habit accuftomed to contemplations
of refinement, in the future progrefs of life, it
will never (without reluctance) exchange its
own approved poffeffions, for lefs valuable, or
unexamined acquifitions.

A great moralift, who had a competent knowledge

ledge of the human heart, and whofe poeti-
cal diction, and ftrength of compofition, would
merit approbation in any age, whofe fentiments
are the language of experience, whofe intimacy
with human nature is fo great, and whofe knowledge of the world is fo ingenioufly introduced
into his writings, that a reader of ordinary pene-
netration muft admire the compafs of his abilities, and even feel the force of his reafoning,
tells us, when the gay feafon of life, in its
various periods, is effectually fecured, to give
credit and belief to the council of wifdom, that
the mind, in every period of its virtuous progrefs, poffeffes the beft caufe for rejoicing, and
will not fail to exhibit the plan of this happy
improvement to the years of maturity, with invariable delight. A continued fenfe of propriety, or a delicate tafte for what is honourable,
makes the foul fhudder at the reality, and even
at the very fhadow, of what is criminal. It is a
fact not to be difputed, that both male and female naturally partake of the prevailing habits
of their company, or the quality of the employ-
ments with which they are moft familiar:
Therefore this leffon of early cultivation is in
                                          itfelf

itfelf fo advantageous, that none fenfible of its ufefulnefs will ever wifh to refift its influence, or think its authority intolerable. The plain injunctions recommended are the very precepts that a judicious parent, concerned for the credit of his family, or the happinefs of a promifing offspring, would fincerely dictate ; and what no children, but fuch as are evidently on the road' to ruin, would ever treat with difdain. Serious impreffions of religion, which comprehend the beft definition of moral beauty, are not only the origin of reputation, but the fountain of uncontaminated pleafure. Improvement in this fage fcience forbids no enjoyment to which common fenfe would give its cônfent, or difcretion defire to poffefs. If the mufical voice of piety was underftood in its proper acceptation, the honour of God regarded, or the dignity of human nature properly fupported, too much care could fcarcely be taken, in the morning of life, to create and encourage the nobleft train of reflections.

This digreffion, the courteous reader, I hope, will not confider as wandering from the main point, or in the leaft lofing fight of the fubject

in

in contemplation. To give as little foundation as poffible to the language of complaint, I fhall here refume the former theme. Is genteel education become an object of particular attention? and is the affection of parents fenfibly awakened to behold the improvement it is able to confer? No criterion can diftinguifh partiality to a favourite more confpicuoufly, than the adorning of her mind with every neceffary beauty, and looking often with a watchful eye at her morals. A female ftands in the fame degree of confanguinity to her connections, is perhaps as capable of receiving inftruction as any of her family, and poffibly makes a brighter figure in the art fhe ftudies; of courfe has the beft claim to an equal fhare of tendernefs and attention. The principal parts of her education, in modern times, confift in French, dancing, drawing, and mufic, and all thefe are highly ornamental, when what is more effential is cultivated with the fame degree of ferioufnefs.

A young female is often hurried to town, and immediately taken to a boarding-fchool, as the centre of every accomplifhment. Here fhe finds new affociates, who require new manners: big

C   with

with every enterprise, and elated with every hope, however vague, the imagination is soon glazed over with the moſt fanciful, as well as the moſt flattering ideas. Chimerical figures of faſhion and empty pageantry, are conſidered as the ſummit of human happineſs. While the judgement is not perfectly ripe, how eaſy for the draughts of fiction to ſteal forward into favour, and by unfair colouring to keep virtues of the firſt quality at an awful diſtance. The gay female enters the world, with every happy prejudice in her favour; ſhe imagines herſelf certain of accompliſhing her purpoſes, and of obtaining the rewards due to eſtabliſhed merit.

When the Sirens of flattery are high in favour, the eye is entertained with whatever they think beautiful; and Vanity's ſickly appetite is regaled with their various delicacies: The treaſures of delight are every where laid open, and novelty blooms alike on every hand.

Thus do the ſmiles of fancy diffuſe their whimſical and unſteady rays, like the ancient Scythians, who, by extending their conqueſts over diſtant regions, left their own throne vacant to their ſlaves. Where prejudices blind the mind, and

the

the fogs of delusion darken the planet of refinement! truth and impartiality are not seen in
their native colours, nor are their instructive
voices distinctly understood. Though the scenes
of happiness lurk under no foreign mask, the
search is often made where only the shadow is
found, and that shadow is without hesitation taken for the substance. The song of hope extends
its enchanting sound, and the inexperienced heart
rejoices in its melody; each day swells with the
reflux of pleasures, variable as the cause from
which they originate.

Those precious hours designed for improvement, are devoted to cards, or other insignificant
pastimes, instead of being usefully employed in
collecting materials of taste, calculated to enlarge
the sphere of refinement, or promote employ-
ments more rational.

The transactions of the day are soon hurried
over. Reflections which require deep penetration are troublesome, and therefore are soon dis-
missed, lest they should sadden the thoughts, and
spoil the appetite for light amusements. A rapid
current of conversation rolls on the milliner, the
mantuamaker, and a numberless group of other

figures,

figures, found neceſſary to employ the tongue
without intermiſſion. Concerts of muſic and public aſſemblies are current courſes of entertainment ; how ſuch a one danced, how elegant her
perſon, what a degree of dignity in her carriage,
but not a ſingle expreſſion about the propriety
of her conduct, or the refinement of her underſtanding. Theſe ſubjects are airy and inſinuating, and the ſchool of meditation, in which
the young female but too much delights. A
latitude of this nature, in connection with a narrow ſet of principles, or a confined view of human nature, cramp the ſpirit of improvement,
and help to encourage ſtrong prepoſſeſſions either
for or againſt matters of no great importance.
In the open unſuſpicious ſeaſon of life, opinions
ſo diſſeminated, are often greedily imbibed. But
having taken root, and being once naturaliſed, it
will require more than an ordinary effort entirely
to eradicate them. In almoſt every age of the
world, it has been leſs or more the practice of phi-
loſophers, poets, and hiſtorians, to laſh the vices
of their time, and complain that moral virtues
were faſt approaching the borders of depravity ;
the uſual cant employed to convince us, that
former

former generations had carried all the spoil of moral improvement, and other valuable blessings, along with them to the land of forgetfulness, and left only the refuse of beauty and taste to their successors. For my part, I cannot say that I am a convert to this opinion; nor do I see any eligible cause for supporting such reasoning. And though, from the liberty I have taken, it may be thought I wish to lay an embargo on the little levities of youth, I hope my sentiments shall not be understood as alluding to the sex at large, nor as comprehending all our females in one class; for I believe the present æra may produce as honest, virtuous, and finished females, as any of the preceding. The ancients, which many seem enthusiastically fond of extolling, I suppose, differed from those of our own time, only by their dress being less handsome, their language less elegant, their integrity less genuine, and themselves less accomplished. In opening the views of the youthful mind, and suggesting subjects of contemplation, caution, in most cases, is quite requisite, not only in the choice of chaste, edifying themes, but also in giving the narration an engaging dress. Innocent and interesting

C 3   anecdotes.

anecdotes might many times be exceeding fea-
fonable, and help to produce a pleafing effect.
The gay colours of vanity, which are fo ready
to inflame, might by fuch habits be gradually
mortified, and the current of thought run with
conftant delight, in the direction of improvement
and happinefs.

Innocent amufement, confined within proper
bounds, is furely requifite; and none in poffeffion
of common fenfe, or who knows the value of
health, will ever difcommend its effect. But to
affign it the place of moral improvement, and
make it the chief object of purfuit, is a piece of
conduct far from deferving credit, or being worthy of encouragement. Life, when regulated
with judgement, is a pleafing fcene, rich with
beauteous decorations, fruitful in acts of benevolence. An hour once a-day devoted to moral
entertainment, would open a door for refinement
and attention to the various occurrences, which
occupy the ruling thoughts of mankind, in their
different attitudes and confequences; would help
to enliven the mind, and lead to a train of ufeful reflections. Inquiry into the quality of virtue, or the deformity of vice, with the lines and
colours

colours peculiar to each; thefe or fimilar lectures would be more than killing time; money
beftowed on a teacher for fuch a purpofe, would
be profitably fpent; the advantages of which
would appear like the ripe increafe of harveft,
in the progrefs of future years. A refpectable
character, whofe name I cannot recollect, ferioufly recommends œconomy of tafte. He is
quite clear for confining friends, as well as books,
to a certain number; defiring but few of either,
if thefe are judicioufly felected. From the merit of the books with which one is familiar, the
turn of the mind is foon difcovered; for tafte
will naturally feek for qualities of its own complexion; as clothes which cover and adorn the body fhould always be genteel, without affectation.
Reading practifed for improvement, and not for
oftentation, will lay up treafures of edifying information, which will entertain the intellect, and
adorn the converfation. Decency in drefs fhews
a delicacy of tafte, and a modeft diffufion of knowledge adds luftre to its fair author. Silence
frequently performs the office of fpeech; and
this fort of eloquence fometimes does more execution than the moft elegant addrefs; like fuf-

penfions

penfions and long paufes in mufic, which contribute as much to harmony as the moft melo-
dious notes. " Glittering wares, if continually
expofed, lofe much of their brightnefs, and are
eafily ftained with much handling." A comely
female, the more natural fhe appears, the more
beautiful; fhe is fure to lofe nothing by the want
of affectation. There would be lefs danger in
meeting her adorned with all the advantages of
drefs, than in feeing her conduct artfully diftinguifhed, by the attractive grace, and delufive
manner of thofe, who have neither had accefs to
good company, nor enjoyed the benefit of a virtuous education.

Modefty is a quality fo acceptable, that it
forms an apology for many deficiences, it is an
armour fcarcely to be pierced, and on a fenfible
female fits very handfomely.

" Diftruftful fenfe with modeft caution fpeaks,
While flattering nonfenfe in full vollies breaks."

 ..lence will act with œconomy in the dif-
      its merit. The difcreet female will ra-
      nt herfelf with having more literary
                              knowledge

knowledge than she chooses to publish, than
that others should cenfure her for affecting more
than she has. She is not clad in her beft suit at
her firft appearance; but thinks it better to gain
ground gradually, than to feem retrograde in her
motions. A judicious female will cheerfully facrifice the light amufement of a dance, the luxury of a repaft, or any other pleafure of the feafon, to tafte fincere and folid enjoyment; by cul-
tivating clofe acquaintance with fome favourite
author, where she finds a lafting feaft prepared
for her mind. I do not think it rafh to cenfure
fome characters, who would be much offended
to have their tafte or judgement difputed, for
maintaining that learning and coquetry in a female are fynonymous terms; and to the em-
bellifhment of education and found fenfe, uncharitably append the epithet of *affectation.*
Though books and their contents are not to employ every hour of the day, the female who is
well acquainted with fuch fenfible neighbours, is
not, in my flender judgement, the lefs qualified
for fprightly converfation. A choice collection
of books, with an inclination to perufe them,
not only fteals away the languor of a dull hour,

but

but ſtrengthens the underſtanding, ʠuickens the apprehenſion, and renders the company of ſo much excellence a fund of agreeable entertainment. But much depends on the quality of the books, with which one enters into a familiar *téte-à-téte*, and the nature of the ſubject on which they treat. The marvellous and fictitious communicate but a ſlender ſhare of pleaſure, their information having no great connection with truth; therefore it is not to be ſuppoſed, that theſe uncertain guides always point to the path of ſecurity ; nay, their courſe is the very reverſe.— Barren uncultivated deſerts are their line of direction, and their falſe colours impoſe on the credulous mind a yoke of deluſion, almoſt equal to Egyptian bondage. And when a taſte for this ſort of reading is once unhappily acquired, a ſtrong effort muſt be made before the reliſh loſes its edge, and the fancy is effectually diſengaged from the falſe ſcenery. Novels, plays, and fables, (excepting a very few indeed), are not productive of the expected inſtruction. But the paſſionate deſire for ſuch paltry productions is perhaps rather a misfortune than a vice ; tho' their prevailing tendency is leſs or more to cloud

the

[35]

the underftanding, with a vain and trivial train of thought, and are a ftrong ftimulation to levity of conduct. The wrong bias, upon the whole, they are calculated to incite, can fcarcely be compenfated by any gratification their fanciful pages can impart. The propenfity which young perfons early difcover to fuch reading, and the partiality they entertain for authors of this defcription, in my eftimation, it would be highly proper to reprefs; and what is much more effential to their welfare, generoufly pointed out, with all the rich advantages which attend its cultivation. Religious and moral performances, are without difpute the folid foundation on which elegance of tafte may be built, and built with fafety. Entertainment of this quality, may be compared to a rich valley, abounding everywhere with correct figures of refinement, fitted both to amufe the eye, and regale the mind. Dr Blair's fermons, are fubjects of deferved fame, and of finifhed beauty; remarkably diftinguifhed by a continued and glowing vein of piety. His tender and inftructive fentiments, in every opening page, are full of nourifhment to virtue; and their elegant language is calculated to gratify the moft refined and delicate

cate tafte. Reforting to fuch polifhed acquaintances, on a Sunday evening, or any other day
of the week that might fuit the reader's conve-
niency, would, in my way of thinking, be a
practice never out of feafon, never inconfiftent
with any character. They are creditable connections; companions with whom any female, whatever be her diftinction in life, may deem it an
honour to be intimate. The divine who ingenioufly gives Piety her fuperlative attire, the
moralift who points out duty with difcernment,
and the hiftorian who paints characters and
events with truth and accuracy, are fuch company as will reflect credit on their affociates.
It is from fuch fources that the principal part of
mental improvement is to be derived. Virtue,
in her natural and moft engaging colours, Vice,
with its gloomy clouds of depravity, with the
characters and confequences peculiar to each, are
fnatched from the jaws of oblivion, and expofed
to public view, for the advantage of fociety, in
the correct and commanding delineation of the
mafterly hiftorian. The annals of barbarous
climates, or of the moft corrupt ages, may, in
fome particular circumftances, appear to be par-
tially

tially tranfcribed, and probably all the tranfactions may not be recollected juft fo minutely as
they were originally exhibited; ftill the principal and leading facts are held up to view in their
narrations, with a tolerable degree of precifion ;
and they feldom lofe fight of truth, or relate
circumftances which are merely chimerical. In
hiftory, a correct fphere of action continually
engages the attention ; you trace the rife and
progrefs of human authority and civilization ;
ages and countries, the interefting affairs of nations, appear as objects of contemplation, and
continually arreft the eye of infpection. The
candid hiftorian fhatters the fecret fetters of ignorance, and, without the leaft referve, lays
open to the glare of day the flourifhing ftate of
empires, or the gradual decay of kingdoms :
together with the various caufes from which
they might date, either the origin of their fame,
or the record of their ruin. The corruption of
the world, and the knowledge of human nature,
may be learned in hiftory without expence, and
feen without a mafk. Whatever error in conduct gave juft room for cenfure, or forfeited
the good opinion of the public, though the ac-

D   tors

tors are now filent, their example continueth to
fpeak. The part entrufted them to execute on
the theatre of life, is recorded with its correfponding portion of merit, or demerit. No concealment of the artful ftratagems, by which in-
flexible integrity often fuffered unexpected difgrace, or undeferved ruin, or by which the natural pride of power rofe up, like a fwelling tor-
rent, to demolifh ftately fabrics of fame, not to
be equalled by fair competition, or the ordinary
means of improvement,—is thought neceffary.
Hiftory gradually unfolds the nature and advantages of different countries; the mildnefs or feverity of climates; the ftrength and intereft of
nations; the rudiments of peace or war; and
whatever concerns civil negotiations: it briefly
comprehends the productions of art, and the
tranfactions of former ages. The different forms
of government, and their various revolutions,
fucceed each other in their natural order. The
multiplied misfortunes which have been the
repeated confequences of too much fecurity or
remiffnefs, extravagant competition, or arbitrary feverity, the fage pages of experience openly
and clearly defcribe. So that no age or nation

can

can lofe credit, by borrowing caution from the
admonition of other countries, and even from
tranfactions not very ancient. The malicious
defigns of bafe minds to foment confufion in a
country, or to kindle the fire of anarchy; the
various deep-coloured artifices by which popular
faction and civil difcords fwelled to rapid inun-
dations; the happy caufes by which the fcent of
dark machinations ftole from retirement, to difcover the fnare, and counteract their horrid influence, before the fecret ripened into age, or
launched into execution; all thefe circumftances
plainly appear, without palliation, or the leaft
apprehenfion of danger. In contemplating the
graceful figures, and amufing fcenery of the
hiftorian, the reader, at a diftance from the field
of danger, may calmly view battles and fieges
without turmoil; tempefts and fhipwrecks, without fharing in the conflict; the modes and
fafhions of other courts and nations, without
either the toil of travelling, or the expence of a
coftly purchafe. In fancy you may proceed to
the field of war, and behold a Cæfar, a Scipio,
and a group of other ancient and modern heroes,
that could eafily be named, with the fortitude of

D 2   foldiers.

foldiers, fupporting fatigue, and communicating courage to all around, by their looks, their addrefs, and their actions, which fly like electricity from rank to rank, till the enthufiafm becomes general, and the effect wholly irrefiftible. You may fee a vanquifhed foe, forgetting the horrors of bondage, and gazing with admiration, on the bravery of the hero, who, with the humanity of an angel, fubdues the proud fpirit of revenge, and, by unexpected clemency, redoubles the obligations he confers. The advantages to be gained by contemplating the judicious arrangement of an army, the manœuvres to be performed, the danger to be avoided, and the meafures to be concerted, are alfo numerous and great.

By hiftory you may be made quite intimate with the moft diftant parts of the globe; may become acquainted with the meafures and treaties, the character and religion, the trade and politics of the Indies, as well as of our own and neighbouring nations. Into the fecrets of ftatefmen you are freely admitted, and thofe actions which it would have been once thought prefumption to oppofe, you may canvafs without referve, you may praife or condemn, agreeable to your

own

own inclination, without either the fear of cenfure, or the imputation of flattery. Thofe principal proceedings may be learned from hiftory,
in one day, which were long in gaining the fum-
mit of *eclat*, and maintained the fame, or agita-
ted the counfels of nations, for a vaft number of
years.

Cardinal Mazarine is one of the fortunate few,
who was greatly beloved, both by prince and
fubject, while living, and who, after his death,
was univerfally regretted.

A monument of no lefs refpect, the Britifh
Cabinet at prefent feems to be foftering, and
bringing forward to maturity. If the fame
uniformity fhould henceforth prevail, that has
hitherto regulated Mr P's. meafures, his
friends will have no caufe to blufh for his
conduct. Let the tongue of candour fpeak, and
the eye of infpection look around;—to fuch
witneffes his merit muft feem great, and to fhine
without an eclipfe. As a financier, how inven-
tive and judicious! Refpecting his abilities as an
orator, the elegance of a Cicero, the ftrength
and reafoning talents of a Demofthenes, he
happily unites in his manly exhibitions.

D 3

The

The chart of life and of hiſtory is a copy of
ſomething more ſerious than fancied novelties :
each feature is big with facts intereſting in their
nature, variegated with extenſive information,
and richly clad with the garb of diſtinction;
more than obliquely treated by the eye of diſ-
cernment, and the ſcientific pen of genius.   In
hiſtory you may cull-the flowers of every virtue, and leave the thorns of miſery to torment
thoſe whoſe complicated follies aroſe to view, in
the deceitful paths of falſe deſire.   When the
game of vice is acted, as it is at all times, and
in every country, though not with the ſame degrees of guilt, the fruit of it will leſs or more
appear, and the recollection return with freſh
aggravation : for the recurrence of ſimilar pre-
miſes cannot fail to produce effects of the ſame
nature., The friendly intention that kindly
marks out the ſavage rocks, on which virtue
and innocence, refinement, fame, and happineſs,
recorded their names and character in the liſt of
thoſe doomed to be unfortunate,—can never be
too highly prized.   In every doubtful ſcene,
buoys are beheld, and with impreſſive eloquence
warn the world of thoſe ſecret dangers and deceitful
                                                 ſhallows

shallows, where levity and indiscretion have frequently felt their folly, and unexpectedly stranded all the ill-calculated treasures of their flattering hopes. You see the cost of lawless gratification, minutely discerned, and faithfully exhibited. An impartial picture of friendship is displayed, and cowardly pretensions to it are stript of their artful plumes: the beautiful colours of sincerity are placed in their proper attitude, and gain the attention of candour and integrity. The conversation of men of letters, who once shone in the walk of literature, you may enjoy as your intimate acquaintances, and with them may talk as familiarly as with your nearest relations. The wise precepts of philosophy, and the just disposition of the colours and figures of rhetoric, you may examine at leisure; and although these lectures should not be so animating to you, as they have been to those who heard their refined authors, in the flow and fire of declamation, still you may enjoy information, mingled with pleasure. Their lives and examples continue yet to charm and to instruct; their inchanting themes are pregnant with moral virtue; and the great beauty that

its

its influence imparts, they felt as well as inculcated; and by so doing, plainly pointed to the
reward by which the uniform progress of virtue and integrity deserve to be distinguished.

The ceremony attending introduction into
company, require, in your closet with your
author, no preparation; nor from a perusal,
if his taste is good, do you run the least risk
of having your morals tainted with depravity.
You have it in your power to chuse your society, and to continue or disengage yourself from
it, just as taste or pleasure may prescribe.
You need not undergo the penance of a dull
anecdote, a tedious narration of trifles, nor the
profane conversation of the profligate; but may
dismiss the haughty and impertinent, without the
least fear of being loaded with the epithet of
prude or coquette. History is a safe companion
to consult; it will enable its favourites to form
their expressions with accuracy, and frame their
actions with judgement. To speak in the language of that elegant, inimitable Poet, Mr
Thomson, " She will, from this standard of
taste, refine her own, correct her pencil to
the purest truth."

A

A habit of reading with proper penetration, not only feizes all the paffes which commonly lead to the avenue of levity, but alfo feafts the mind with delicacies, quite remote from the amufement collected from vulgar prejudices, or flovenly expreffions. From the plain recital of thefe incidents, we may eafily perceive how highly ufeful it is to be well acquainted with hiftory, and how richly it contributes to improve the converfation. Thus the amufement of reading, while regulated with judgement, will at once polifh the thoughts, refine the underftanding, and convey wifdom to the heart, through the medium of pleafure.

The prefent mode of education, I fhould think, would fuffer no depreciation from ferious and frequent attempts to embellifh the youthful mind, with a tafte for internal ornament, as well as external decorations; and to direct the principal part of their application, in the opening bloom of life, to the adorning of their judgement with the fair garb of virtue. Moral beauty, early and carefully cultivated, kindly diffufes over the foul, in every period of life, the funfhine of deferved fame, and unclouded happinefs.

Voter

Votes of approbation, may be fecured by falfe
means, but their credit will not be long maintained, unlefs they are fupported by a firmer
foundation. The gems of religion, though they
may not have the fame beauty to every eye, are
not the lefs valuable upon that account; the
artift, without the help of either a touch ftone
or a microfcope, can diftinguifh the genuine from
the counterfeit. Perhaps candour and truth are
in no eafe more neceffary, than in examining
propofitions where the intereft of religion is
concerned; but if treated with the impartiality
fuitable to her character, fhe has nothing to fear
from the clofeft inveftigation. Some countenances are covered with more than common attrac-
tion, and are formed at once to awaken furprife,
and to fecure virtue againft the hoftile attempts
of malice and rudenefs. Beauty is ever accompanied with genuine fimplicity; whofe unaffected features are fo plain and engaging, that the
fair actrefs fteals upon the heart infenfibly, and
every where produces a welcome emotion. The
choice flowers of innocence and virtue, have expreffions of tafte, not only in the finery of their
foliage, but every fibre is full of fignificance,
and

and pregnant with some valuable quality.
Religion, in her simple artless attire, though she
stoops not slavishly, nor conforms her mode to
the fashion of every fancy, is not on that account
the less respectable. The homage of her friends
is a tribute of unforced devotion, the prejudices
of her foes make them repine at the sight of
her unusual banner; but the umbrage she cannot completely remove, she in some measure,
reduces to silence. Her aspect is pleasant and
joyful, as the noon-day sun; and the serenity of
heaven smiles in her look. Her voice is full of
harmony, with the breathings of humanity;
she enters not into private connection with the
thunder-bolts of hostility, nor ever gives her
sanction to indecent feuds: Thus the proclama-
tions of the Christian scheme roll away our
fears, like noisy waves, to die before us on the
shore of hope. Her face of love is no glimmer-
ing taper of uncertain ray, that points to paths
of doubtful termination, or that leads to the
lonely walk of delusive superstition; but the
bright effulgence of eternal splendour, durable
and fair as its Almighty Author, To finish the
description,

defcription, I fhall quote the words of a polite, as well as a Chriftian poet.

> Believe the mufe, the wintry blaft of death,
> Kills not the buds of virtue; no they fpread
> Beneath the heavenly beam of brighter funs,
> Through endlefs ages into higher powers!

Religion was prefcribed to the human fpecies, as a neceffary rule of duty, in the early dawn of creation, as well as to every fucceeding age: and whatever part of ancient records we chufe to glance over, we fhall find, that in every climate or nation, where its generous influence was oppofed, where its authority has been degraded, and its friendly vifits coldly admitted, rudely entertained, or forced to depart, cruelty and ignorance have immediately reared their ferpentine heads, and barbarifm opened the way for an influx of favage manners, to occupy the deferted ftation of its heavenly form. But where the religion which is from above, pure and peaceable, lays open her beauty to the gazing eye, like a good picture executed with a mafterly hand, fhe will difplay her colours with a particular luftre. To every individual, as well as to every community, fhe adds a gracefulnefs

that

that is truly divine; for she is the very
sinew of beauty and health. "Length of days
"are in her right hand, and in her left, riches
"and honour; her ways are ways of pleasant-
"nefs, and all her paths are peace." She is the
parent of felicity, and the guardian of innocence.
Profperity and pleafure look best in her drefs,
and adverfity derives its only confolation from
her refreshing cordials. Her counfel is that of
an angel, and the fymphonious notes with which
she delights to entertain her principal favourites,
are fweeter than the mufic of paradife. The
ftructure of her felicity bends not before the
blafts which affail it; her radiant intellectual
light banishes the gloom of terror, and elevates
the mind with increafing comfort, as we draw
nigh the climate of eternal day. Our Saviour
tells us, "that his yoke is eafy, and that his
"burden is light;" and religion is furely fo, to
thofe who shall literally imbibe its fpirit. To
declaim againft all innocent amufement, bears a
ftronger fcent of Pharifaical cant, than of Chriftian moderation. It requires neither philofophi-
cal difquifitions, nor acute reafoning, to convince
us, that the gofpel of the world will fometimes

E   act

act with a feverity quite inconfiftent with that Chriftian charity which covers the facred oracles with confummate beauty. Religion, as explained by our Saviour and his difciples, confifts not in a diftortion of countenance, in a cloud of ill-nature refting on the brow; nor in feclufion from focial intercourfe, as if piety fhould have exiftence no where elfe, but in cells and cloifters:—no fuch facrifices are required by it ; it only forbids guilty gratifications, or that licentious inclination which boldly fets all laws, both human and divine, at defiance. To rational delight, religion can never be an enemy, for it is the honeft good heart that has the beft title to enjoy contentment ; and to refufe happinefs to the truly virtuous, and transfer it to the profane, would be equally irrational and unjuft. The foolifh flights of levity, or the dangerous excurfions of impiety, to which a violation of facred rites may eafily waft its giddy votaries, are too often practifed by the fons of inconfideracy. Thefe gracelefs figures feldom fpeak in the ftyle of devotion. Their acquifitions are not a collection of jewels, nor treafures capable of purchafing refinement of morals, or peace of mind.

mind. The perfons who deal deepeft in artifice, affume frequently an air quite oppofite to their eftablifhed habits. And as they know themfelves in fome meafure deftitute of natural means, they attempt to fupply the deficiency by counterfeit ones; and to accomplifh their purpofes, they fuit their language and manner as much to the character they affect as poffible: For hypocrify is a character which vice dares not avow; and a forced homage, which, however unwilling, it muft pay to virtue, and which virtue, without difpute, is entitled to obtain. A few may admire thofe artful actors who can affume all the gay colours of the rainbow, with an equal facility; but integrity will fecure efteem, and be fupported with fuccefs, when the filly artifices of diffimulation fhall meet with merited contempt. Rich flowers communicate to their familiar affociates a fragrant and refrefhing flavour; in like manner, fhe who wifely difcerns the beauties of divine improvement, will naturally ftudy to acquire them; and will uniformly emit the grateful odour of a good example: for when once effectually initiated in virtue, the impreffion will not only remain in

full

full force, but from day to day gain her refpect, extend her conquefts, and increafe her intellectual beauty. Modefty, truth, and virtue,
in their unaffected robes, not only invite the eye
of admiration, but make the perfon poffeffed of
fuch fuperlative properties enjoy the ferenity
of heaven; refulgent beams of felf-approbation
ever fmile on the dome, diftinguifhed by ornaments fo engaging; no foaming billows difturb
her joy, no rifing tempeft clouds her profpect,
who is endued with difcretion, and in whofe
breaft moral beauties take up their abode.
Be affured, fays a fenfible writer, that no character is more amiable, than that of a female;
who, in the gay feafon of life, and in the triumph
of beauty, practifes the known rules of felf-go-
vernment, and whofe correct tafte, and fenfible
manner, publifh at once, that her religion is
much more than an obfolete term, or a flafhy
oftentation.

A light-houfe is a metaphor, (though fomewhat coarfe), that conveys an idea of fecurity;
religion, in like manner, points to the deceiving
banks, and treacherous rocks, which promife
nothing but danger and ruin. Therefore it is

perfectly

perfectly requifite to have a careful look-out, in
the narrow channel, and on a lee-fhore; for it
is by efcaping the rifk of thefe, and the boi-
fterous ocean, that landing is attended with fuch
fingular degrees of happinefs.

The giddy and the thoughtlefs may behold
the ferene afpect of religion, the unfafhionable-
nefs of her manner, the circumfpection of her
behaviour, with contempt or indifference; for
the facrifices fhe requires may feem difficult,
and the reftraints fhe impofes exceeding great:
But if the beauties which compofe the Chriftian
character be an object of choice, the duties it
enjoins will appear neceffary and reafonable.
Refpect to its facred obligations, is greatnefs
indeed; and in the conftant and rational exercife
of religion, good breeding, as well as found fenfe,
are exemplified, and beautify the character more
eminently than robes of filk.

A judicious officer will feldom rank his beft
men in front, or expofe them to the firft onfet,
but make choice of the moft eminent for a *corps*
of referve. The mafterly hiftorian, the artful
poet, and the fkilful painter, clofe their delineations with the fineft colours, and make their

heroine

heroine, or hero, appear in the moſt engaging
poſition, juſt at the finiſhing ſtroke.

Suppoſe the education of the young female
now complete, the boarding tutoreſs giving her
laſt benediction in the ſtyle of motherly affection,
and the ripe information of years and experience,
reſerving the ſtrength of her counſel to the con-
cluding ſcene, it would perhaps conſiſt of ſentiments ſimilar to the following. " You have
already experienced a ſufficient proof of parental
regard, and how great a ſhare of their affection
your happineſs has conſtantly engaged. Whatever appeared requiſite to advance your improvement, or contribute to your felicity, met
with a willing and liberal ſupport. Obligations
have been beſtowed with ſo much generoſity,
that I perſuade myſelf, your gratitude will ex-
preſs itſelf in every part of your future conduct,
and effectually convince them, that you have been
looking after ornaments of greater value than
the fluctuations of faſhionable dreſs ; and that
their partiality, in reſpect to you, has not in one
ſingle point been miſplaced." The gloſs that
heightens the natural charms of modeſty, is effectually deſtroyed, when expoſed with eagerneſs

to

to every paffing eye. Men always admire the
cautious female, whofe wifdom feems to tell the
ftranger, I give you leave to guefs who I am.
A proper eftimation of circumftances, and of
living manners, (the diftinguifhed feature of her
who has had accefs to company, and the benefit
of a proper education), is not only health, and
fecurity to the foul, but tends to unfetter the
mind from the confufed clouds of illiberal prejudices, and in fome meafure to deftroy the effect of felfifh habits.

A female in the bloom of beauty, entering
into the world, has the engaging profpect of
various enjoyments, preffing forward to her
view, and rifing around her in thick fucceffion.
Her morning gay, her hopes alive, and her fuccefs in life feemingly fecure. No furly tempefts
appear; all is friendfhip and favour; and to
falute her fprightly form, happinefs from every
avenue rufhes forward in hafte. But the gloom
of difappointment fometimes unexpectedly fucceeds. The fun of hope grows dim, and the
tumult of the ocean is heard; though this fhould
not be the cafe, fhe furely bids faireft for happinefs, who looks with penetration into every
opening

opening event, and is always with caution preparing for a storm. What has the finest female
in poffeffion, that can authorife her to nurfe
pride, or cherifh vanity? Her body at the beft
is feeble, and every moment of life fubject to
difeafes and death. In her colour and complexion, in drefs and elegance, the very flowers
of the field outfhine her. In the fulleft bloom
of beauty, how eafily and unexpectedly may a
change be effected! The moft engaging form,
even from a few hours ficknefs, may receive a
very different afpect.

"What is the blooming tincture of a fkin,
To peace of mind and harmony within?
What the bright fparkling of the fineft eye,
To the foft foothing of a calm reply?
Can comelinefs of form, or fhape, or air,
With comelinefs of words, or deeds compare?
No, thofe at firft, the unwary heart may gain,
But thefe, thefe only, can the heart retain."

A female of diftinction and merit requires
the application of the mental pick, as much as
one who moves in a folitary unfrequented fphere.
The former, like a bright ftar of confiderable
magnitude,

magnitude, dazzles with her intellectual accomplishments, no less than by her external finery; and from the united efforts of these singular embellishments, her temptations are not more various, than her conquests are extensive. Vanity may chance to infinuate herself by the deceitful artifices of flattery; and by her soft enchantments, strengthen the velocity of the passions, and provoke their appetite to the pursuit of enjoyments, sometimes not easily attained; but to which the wing of fancy, or a vague wish, may frequently extend. The alluring marks of distinction which wealth and fame bestow, raise admiration every where; and she who shines most in these plumes, is thought the peculiar favourite of fortune; but solid judgement will penetrate through the disguise, and discover that the greatest flow of affluence does not continually chain happiness to the gilded dome. She whose mind is much inflamed, or estimates her merit from the weight of her money, would find her interest promoted by just reflections on the various objects which claim so much of her respect. Let her calmly consider, that her riches are but small, when compared with those of Cræsus;

and

and yet that the name of Solon alone could incite Cyrus to grant him a reprieve, which all
his wealth was unable to purchafe. She who
feels impulfive elation from the highnefs of her
birth, or the rank of her family, ought to annex to each of thefe articles, their natural fignificance; and as thefe are diftinctions not of her
acquiring, a few ferious reflections will eafily
rectify the diforder, and expofe the impropriety
of attempting to eftablifh continued fame on fuch
infirm foundations. The female who can fhew
no merit, but what fhe borrows from her parents or pedigree, is much obliged to her anceftors, but can never expect the fame degree of
fincere approbation.

A female of correct tafte would fcorn to efti-
mate her character by counterfeit figns of merit.
She will join the Grecian exclamation, " It is
difhonourable for Sparta to fly, but noble to conquer."

She knows too well, that to flutter on the
wings of her friend's reputation or fortune,
would be to ftipulate her own merit at a very
low value; therefore, like a true chemift, fhe

endeavours

endeavours to make the proper use, without
over-rating these advantages.

She analyzes the quality of complex materials,
and philosophically reduces their value to the
primitive standard. She will allow the world
its riches, honours, and pleasures, and with the
nicest discernment observes, that these have neither any fixed duration, nor wholly exempt their
proprietors from trouble. In the circle of her
own acquaintances, she beholds beauty perish in
its bloom, ambition sink in its triumph, and,
from the public news, sees every day fresh in-
stances of riches deprived of their pride, and
new graves opened for younger and older than
herself. The language of these lectures is no
feeble effort of eloquence; the truths repeated
are strong and important, and feelingly recommend the model on which the fair female should
form her conduct. The love of fame animates
the exertions of those who entertain high
thoughts of the dignity of human nature; and
when that spirit is once effectually imbibed, it
will carry on the prosecution of its schemes, till
they terminate either in pleasing success, or sad
disappointment.

In

In the breaft where prudence fecures the
priority of place, no compulfion is requifite to
enforce the benefit of propofitions, which need
no fupport from ftrength of argument, or depth
of reafoning; having truth for their foundation,
and happinefs for the end at which they aim.
The mental pick is fo convenient an inftrument,
that it may eafily be carried about, without the
leaft offence to either friends or foes : its regifter
is a kind of day-book, where accounts may be
fairly ftated; and a juft computation of the
fmall fums which are often neglected, and what
they would amount to, if managed agreeable to
the rules of œconomy, might no doubt prove
ferviceable. For characters of the firft rate are
not fo perfect; but lefs or more improvement
might be made. The female of correct tafte,
has penetration fufficient to reflect on the quality
of virtue, and the various favours fhe is capable
of beftowing. She perceives that her credit
procures every where the falutation of refpect;
that her own confequence is eftablifhed, in proportion to the relation in which fhe ftands to a
connection fo honourable; a connection, that not
only reflects inimitable luftre on her name and
. family,

family, but enables her, when she retires from
the gay crowd, to enjoy the serenity of solitude,
and to peruse the volume of her own heart without the blushes of remorse. A valuable prize,
in all ages and countries, has been thought a
motive sufficient to produce abundance of com-
petitors: and what acquisition can equal an un-
sullied reputation? a prize which can only be
gained by the diligent improvement of moral
beauties. She who has once effectually acquired
the art of standing in awe of herself, stands in
no need of Seneca's imaginary tuition; for if she
is capable of knowing herself, she will be capable of correcting her errors; and would rather
fall from the Tarpeian rock, than from the alti-
tude of discretion. A portrait of such finished
features, is a model of beauty, and a living book
of unquestionable merit. Modesty in behaviour,
as well as judgement in taste, invite the contemplation of the judicious, to behold arrangement
and painting of no fictitious decorations. A capacity to chuse, and chuse well, belongs only to
the ingenious and discerning; it is indeed great
skill to know what is truly beautiful. The sa-
gacious female, who is scientifically inclined, and

F   has

has learned to retire often within the fanctuary of filence, and to meditate deliberately on her own intereft, in every fphere of life, will reap the rich increafe of her wifdom, and be adorned in a manner quite different from the artificial embellifhments of pride and vanity. The beauties of piety and truth, treafured up in the female breaft, can fcarcely be affected by any event, nor fpoiled by the ravages of time. The rudenefs of accidents may impair her health, or hurt her fortune; but can never injure her fame. She has got the key of beauty, as well as of happinefs, who loves virtue, and daily purfues the path of integrity. This is the fource of improvement, from whence all that is good and lovely proceeds; and a mark of diftinction, fuperior to all the titles of dignity, that Rome, in her moft flourifhing ftate, could either invent or confer. Beauty, a ftranger to the artifices neceffary to fupport the influence, or preferve the fame, of external elegance, refembles the alluring fign of fome eminent merchant, which courteoufly invites the ftranger to ftep in to his fhop, where he finds every thing within, correfponding to the outward appearance: were he

deceived,

deceived, indeed, he would leave it as foon as he could with decency, make the beft of his way home, and banifh all thoughts of a future vifit.

Feelings of a delicate nature can have no great pleafure in affociating with thofe of an oppofite texture. Their manner, action, tafte, fentiment, and language, have fo much of a contrariety, that a fincere or lafting agreement, or genuine happinefs, can fcarcely be expected from a fcene of fuch motley inconfiftencies. The female who is emulous to excel, who wifhes to remain in poffeffion of herfelf, will never ftoop to the artful ftrains of vanity, nor greedily fwallow the low delufive language of flattery ; which tends to endanger her difcretion, and deprive her of other fenfible enjoyments. For when once the heart and ear are engaged on the fide of fuch fubtile deceivers, the difpofition will foon change its natural fweetnefs, the imagination immediately fwell, and be quite intoxicated with airy expectations. Not only fhall mental improvement be ftopt, and goodnefs of heart hindered to operate, the vail of modefty fhall be dropt, and colours affumed, flattering as thofe of the

F 2   rainbow,

rainbow, but equally fluctuating. For she who
is so unhappy as to evade the counsels of wisdom, and the salutary injunctions of religion,
quits at once her connection with happiness,
friendship, merit, and a character with herself
and the world. Whereas the cautious female
not only successfully overcomes temptations,
but rejoices in the fruits of her victory:. She
selects with judgement the kind of arms proper
to be used, and necessary to win the field. Her
mind and her eyes are equally attentive to the
destructive excursions of profaneness, and the giddy flights of unhallowed levity: she sees what
they are, and views them as enemies, with
which she is determined to enter into no terms
of reconciliation; and whoever attempts to make
their gilded bait sweet to her taste, she considers
as those who have a design on her happiness.
The first psalm is an elegant mirror for improvement; and by a substitution of the feminine
gender, may admit of the following unlaboured
comment. "Perfect happiness awaits her, who
in the counsel of the ungodly walketh not a-
stray; who envyeth not the way of sinners, nor
delights to stand in their rank. The scorner's
chair

chair she will never occupy, nor laugh at those who do: her character may be compared to a tree, planted by a river in a fertile soil, whose leaf shall never fade, but in due season yieldeth abundance of rich fruit." While the smiles of prosperity continue to shine, and successfully extend their flattering rays, then religion may possibly appear to disadvantage; her breath may become languid, and her figure unengaging; and to get rid of her troublesome importunity, means and measures are always ready at hand.

Cardinal Woolsey, prime minister to Henry the Eighth, by his own pitiful confession, has left upon record an example of the woful consequences of exchanging the important duties of devotion, for considerations of infinitely less value. How melancholy and affecting his exclamation, when approaching the verge of the grave, " Alas! alas!" said he, " what a fall of fortune! had I been only half as faithful in the service of my God, as I was in that of my king and country, I am persuaded he would neither have neglected nor despised me, in my feeble declining days." But the sympathetic feelings are relieved from the struggle of commiseration,

F 3   by

by reflecting on the manly piety of the following character. The Duke of Portland being somewhat late, it is said, one morning in coming to the *levee*, King George the Second, with his courtiers around him, saluted him with a smile, as he stepped into the drawing-room, " There you come, smoking from your prayers." " I blush not at the observation, nor am in the least ashamed to own it. And I am confident, that your Majesty will not think me the less loyal subject, for paying my respects, and bending my knee *first* to the King of kings." A heroic reply from a martial spirit; but however bright this example may appear, we have a much higher to contemplate. The Lord's Prayer is a model without its equal; every expression is inimitably beautiful, and rich with instruction. It is an abridgement of the whole Christian system; its lessons are plain and pious; it is the breath of benevolence, and the language of heaven. These short, but sublime articles of faith, under which the extent of our duty is comprehended, can never be too much regarded. Serious and frequent perusal of this finished copy, with an intention to benefit by its healthy

direction,

direction, has, in every ſtation and ſtage of life, a cloſe connection with happineſs. It not only enjoins equity, and the ſpirit of forgiveneſs and humanity, in our prevailing purſuits, but it is alſo like a guardian angel, or a perpetual *memento*, againſt the inſinuating arts of temptation.

Thus we may ſuppoſe the concluſion of her advice, not more ſincere, than ſtrongly impreſſed with the emphaſis of religion, and the energetic beauties of virtue. Having ſo far revealed her mind to her ward, and faithfully diſcharged her truſt, the governeſs allows her full liberty to purſue her journey home-wards, with the additional wiſh of much happineſs, and a joyful meeting with her family and friends. It may reaſonably be thought, that the particular attention paid to her education, in the different branches of uſeful knowledge, and the leſſons frequently preſcribed, for the regulation of her future conduct, have been ſo much to the purpoſe, that any further obſervations on the ſubject might be deemed either arrogant or unneceſſary.

But if I thought my perſevering in the matter
ter

ter would not be conftrued into an offence, nor
deferve the epithet of idle words, I would proceed a little further; and if my ftyle and mode of
difcuffion fhould not impart much information,
I fhall endeavour to fupply the deficiency by
the fpirit of meeknefs. That a fubject of this
nature would require a greater degree of intimacy with the human heart, and a larger ftock
of experience and knowledge, than with decency I can claim, is a difcovery which I ftand
in no need of being told; for I am already perfectly fenfible of the fecret. But as I am not
out of conceit with female beauty, nor ever
wifh to be, the ftandard of the virtuous character, I muft own, is the banner of credit I
fhould wifh if poffible to reach. And though
her caufe fhould not receive much juftice from
fo unpolifhed a pencil, I hope at leaft it has been
and will be my fincere defire, that whatever refpect fhe meets with, vice fhall have none.

Whatever may be the ftage on which we are
to appear, a graceful introduction is a principal
key to the fpectator's affection, and tends greatly to overturn his prejudices againft an accomplifhed actrefs. Great expectations are always

ways formed from the firſt appearance, and the more natural the exhibition, the pleaſure muſt be felt in proportion. The voice of applauſe always flows eaſy, when a compliment is ſupported with ſincerity, and is not the effect of forced complaiſance.

She who brightens like the noon-day ſun, and dazzles moſt when the ſcene ſeems darkeſt; who, in the ſtation ſhe occupies, diſorders no feature with ſhame or confuſion; who loſes not a particle of her merit, but ſteadily keeps it up, and continually gains as ſhe advances, has a fair and juſt title to the palm of honour. She may view it without a bluſh, and wear its encircling wreath upon her brow with conſcious approbation.

A juſt eſtimation of any character cannot be made by a ſingle glance, but in order to procure a correct opinion, various views are neceſſary; and if its beauties continue unclouded and equal, when obſerved in various poſitions, the reſult of the contemplation muſt lead to deſerved homage; eſpecially where natural uniformity, genuine taſte, and correct judgement, are found ſtrongly and often to co-operate.

Chriſtina,

Chriſtina, to the advantages of education and ſtrong ſenſe, adds a choice taſte, and a ſingular ſhare of modeſty. To models of refinement, ſhe is always attentive; and ſtudies to copy beauties ſeparated from rubbiſh, as much as poſſible: for imitation, without diſcerning ſome flower of elegance, is only carrying a taper, for expoſing folly more clearly to notice. To perſonate a character, or adopt a part where the features are all counterfeited, and different from the original, is a diſguiſe that ſoon betrays the imperfect actor it would artfully conceal. If elegant language, poliſhed periods, and an affable manner, ſhould captivate or engage one's taſte, when covered with a maſk; the charms which theſe create will rather augment than hinder the expoſure of a correſponding beauty; and if any ſhould think it convenient to aſſume the ſhadow of any virtue, the poſſeſſion of its reality muſt be much more deſirable; for it inſpires equanimity of mind, and excludes that ſort of tremour, or fear of detection, which is the inſeparable attendant of impoſition.

Whatever is natural in itſelf gains no advantage from dark wavering clouds, unleſs it

be

be in the comparifon, where the inferiority of
the one makes the brightnefs of the other more
confpicuous. The gracefulnefs that will always
pleafe, never drags any of the tawdry performances of diftempered fancy to the face of light;
for its inherent influence, confifts in uniform
wealth of mind, and ftanding habits of virtue,
brought forth in the nurfery of ingenious difcernment, and reared to maturity by a fincere and
continued connection with the fpirit of moral
and divine improvement. The plain honeft
colours of integrity, without any varnifh or
artificial aid, have a beauty quite correct,
altogether fuperior to the paltry trappings of
diffimulation. She who expects to enjoy the
refined entertainment, that forms no connection
with future anxiety, will find her intereft in
making the 'fphere of her innocence as fecure as
poffible; for the accomplifhments of an angel
cannot be acquired, without particular attention
to the duties which compofe the character.
The manner of the politician may have its admirers, and be thought the effect of knowledge
and experience, notwithftanding of the character to which fome annex it. Chriftina's conversation,

verfation, in the principal parts of fpeech, is, like her gestures, quite natural, and richly coloured with mental beauties. Therefore fhe will never facrifice the honourable accents of truth, to the pliable ftyle of finefle, nor feem defirous to pleafe her companions, by quitting the character of integrity. She has beauties peculiar to herfelf; but her peculiarity is not fo much obferved in the order of her drefs, as in the improvement of her mind. She has penetration fufficient to remark the advantages to be derived from reading, and the entertainment which ufeful books impart. She keeps her eyes open to behold her own actions; and effectually perceives, that no book requires more frequent perufal, than the volume of her own life, and the picture which her prevailing actions exhibits. She is never averfe to felf-infpection; her own heart is frequently examined, and with its various emotions fhe is well acquainted.

Every performance noted for its value, fhe treats with filent refpect; and whatever is otherwife, fhe is not only anxious to remove, but to have the vacancy filled with fome choice fubftitute. Thus, from a conftant repetition of improvements,

provements, so conducive to happiness, she is in a fair way of accumulating more than a common stock of intellectual riches, and of giving her pleasures a more poignant zest, than the languid enjoyments of the miser, or the gross entertainments of the prodigal.

That a good heart, and the breathings of humanity, are first-rate ornaments, which claim every where the throne of affection, and embellish handsomely the station which they occupy, are discoveries which Christina will readily admit; for to meditation and inspection she is no stranger.

But the manner or foibles of her acquaintances, are not the materials which compose the train of her amusements, or form the chief subjects of her study.

Attentively she reflects on her own character, as she stands connected with society, and the public view to which she is exposed. She knows the nature of the part in which she is engaged, is serious and important; and examines the power of the causes, as well as the progress of every effect, with nice discerning, and impartial criticism. She is not in the least backward in

G   her

her inquiry, as to the figure she herself makes
in the present sphere of existence; nor as to the
character with which she appears in the register
of heaven, or the colour that her name and
actions will deserve and bear, in the opinion of
succeeding ages. A building erected with plain
materials, of a solid substance, regularly conducted, and closely cemented, is always less
chargeable, than the unsettled, insufficient, ill-
constructed edifice: for the fabric that is founded
on a rock, and bears in every corner the character of connection and strength, requires no
security or out-works for its support. Thus
Christina trembles for no eye; her hand holds
out no bribe to the witnesses of her folly; she
claims no patch of concealment for any part of
her character; for irregularity never forces the
intrenchments of her virtue and honour. Her
laurels are not like the spoil of conquerors, pur-
chased at the expence of planting misery in the
corner from which they had been violently
snatched; but the brightness of innocence, and
the trophies of deserved fame; the texture is
extraordinary, and the quality durable: like
Aaron's rod, if I may be allowed the compari-
son,

son, producing unfading blossoms, and fruit fully
ripe, rich to the taste, and pleasing to the eye.
In other articles, as well as those already mentioned, sensibility and decency will in a great
measure regulate her taste. She will easily
learn from the practice of inventors, or those
who have a novelty in their manner; who, like
the post-boy, carry a budget of news continually
about with them; and deal out their fustian stuff,
either wholesale or retail, as occasion may serve.
But although prating and defamation are less
or more the weeds of every soil, and the misfortune to which the best of characters are very
often exposed, Christina is so far from joining
in their rude vociferation, that she pauses for
recollection, and finds that she has defects of her
own, which, though she does not treat with the
partiality of favourites, effectually repress her
propensity to slander.

Thus, while she is conscious of inability in
herself to reach conspicuous virtue, she sincerely sympathises with others engaged in a
similar struggle. She knows that detraction, in
every age, has had religion and philosophy for
its enemies: And as it is by no means the man-

G 2   ner

her by which merit is made vifible, fhe is fure
to purchafe no part of her amufement at fuch a
price. She is quite fenfible, that when a perfon
has once found the way of being well employed at home, the difficulty of refifting the
fpirit, which aims at croping the reputation of
others, or which feems to delight in illiberal
reflections, will gradually leffen, and at length
evanifh.

Detractors are tutors who will inftruct their
pupils *gratis*, and often in fecrets which they
ought to conceal. When the inquifition of malice begins to operate, a cloud of imaginary
•foibles are eafily invented; but a fenfible female
will never feed the flame of ill nature. The
rage of prejudice, fhe will ftrive to conquer, as
difcretion may dictate. The garb of hoftility,
and the thunder-bolts of revenge, fhe never
meets in a fimilar form; but counteracts their
influence by the fpirit of mildnefs, and the fmiles
of civility. The odious vice of detraction is
thus fenfibly expofed by a finifhed pencil.
" When the colours of calumny are once un-
furled, volunteers flock to her ftandard, multi-
tudes form her camp, for want of better em-
ployment;

ployment; and flying fquadrons are difperfed every where, fo well pleafed with the opportunity of mifchief and pillage, that they toil without profpect of treafure, without hope of profit. But whatever may be the motive of their conduct, it is beft to overlook it : for folly fcarcely can deferve refentment, and malice is punifhed by negled," If veracity was always to meet with indulgence agreeable to its quality, duplicity would never be in vogue ; it would juftly be confidered as rubbifh, of which common fenfe fhould be afhamed ; and a meannefs quite unworthy of entertainment. The language of truth is fafe and graceful ; the blufhes of confufion, and the colouring of fhame, are at no time the effect of its grateful accents. It changes not with circumftances, nor does it grow decriped with age. In fhort, it is the effence of all beauty, and the beft letter of recommendation, that any can carry in their company. A difcourfe or converfation, darkly clouded with the counterfeit of truth, or the acrimonious remarks of the fatirift, as the chofen figures of rhetoric,— effectually banifhes the enjoyment of pleafure, and the quality of beauty. Decency in manner or

G 3   expreffion,

expreffion, fhows refinement of fentiment, and a delicacy of thought, happily feafoned with the advantages of acute difcerning. Injurious liberties, in either language or practice, difcovers a barbarous mind, and betrays great want of tafte.

Chriftina's perceptions are always deeply tinctured with the beauties of truth; into whofe place fhe will admit no fubftitute, however fair or flattering. And thofe deftitute of fuch qualities, are none of her favourites, and but feldom fharers in her amufements: before fhe fixes her friend or acquaintance, fhe takes notice of their deportment, looks to the natural conftruction of their character, and in matters of fuch importance to her happinefs, trufts no eyes but her own. In her retrofpect of paft events, fhe finds names upon record, that will be tranfmitted to future ages, with thofe ftains of reproach which adhere only to the worft of characters, to thofe who wound under fair profeffions of affection; but when perfons of this defcription appear, fhe wifely views their deceitful countenance, as a dangerous coaft fhe is not to approach. When fhe receives money, fhe fenfibly

fibly proves its quality, for she knows, in case she does not challenge the imposition in its season, she may chance to suffer for her credulity. Her friend she will view with equal precision; and as Euripides says of truth, that it loves plain language, affection, in like manner, should be sincere and genuine, without any connection with the variegated colours of cloudy dissemblance.

As she is cautious in the choice of her friend, she is also composed in her devotion, serious and punctual in her duty to her Maker. Respect to whatever is sacred, is her Sunday and daily disposition. She modestly attends the temple of her God; and her intention in appearing there, is not so mean a motive as popular applause, or the outward colour of religion; her decent manner and sober gait, which are neither borrowed nor artificial, will express something more amiable. She observes a line of conduct quite different from that which prevails at a ball, a theatre, or any other scene of amusement, where false pleasure sparkles in every eye, and a constant succession of compliments are every where exchanged. Her opinion

nion is not solely supported from its being the practice of the country where she resides; nor does it arise from the vain fancy of being noticed for the elegance, or peculiar quality of her dress. These are not her ruling causes of repairing to the house of devotion. The solemnity of her manner will repeat her business, and the impression she entertains will merit all due respect. She piously considers it as a place consecrated to the worship of her God, venerable from age, and calculated to influence her mind with a dutiful sense of the obligations she is under, and which she thinks herself bound to recognise. She not only studies to maintain a serious frame, suited to the external rites she countenances, but also a modification of manner, sufficient to overawe the wandering sallies of fancy, with this seasonable reflection, that the incense offered by the lips is altogether unprofitable, and an insult to the Deity, unless the heart sincerely joins in the sacred service. If the composition has taste enough to merit approbation, she will not churlishly with-hold her tribute of praise: If otherwise, her practice will indicate more of the Christian, than to join with the ill-natured

in

in their illiberal farcafms. Thefe are fome of
the beauties of Chriftina's character.

To do as we wifh to be done by, our Saviour
makes the principal point on which the authority of the law and the prophets was wholly
eftablifhed. Univerfities are not the only places
to which we fhould repair, with a view to learn
the obligations of virtue. The inclofures of
erudition are not the infallible fanctuary we
are to explore for a decifion, correfponding to
the logical defcriptions we may hear of moral
duties. The lectures of the philofopher, in the
glowing colours of his expreffive delineation,
may pleafe the tafte, and charm the ear : his
choice inftructions may be continually feafoned
with uncommon figures of rhetoric, ftrength of
reafoning, elegance of language, and harmony
of periods. Such fubjects, no doubt, even in
rehearfal or fpeculation, are both edifying and
entertaining : yet it is the practice alone that
claims the greateft fhare of approbation, and
effectually determines the character.

Ordinary capacities can eafily diftinguifh beauty from deformity; no depth of penetration is
required to mark the natural features of each.

Virtue

Virtue and vice have ever been at variance; and no argument has yet been found powerful enough to produce a reconciliation. Where the mandates of divine truth are oppofed, and propriety of morals laid afide, or carelefsly overleaped, there lawlefs appetites are fure to rife and rage: and when that is the cafe, the fate of virtue may eafily be figured; for whoever purchafes illicit gratifications at the expence of duty and difcretion, is fure to over-rate his enjoyments. But the progrefs of virtue is always fteady, and free from the tumult of paffion or confufion; therefore, in order to fecure felicity, meafures antecedent or in alliance with happinefs, muft be uniformly adopted.

A failor, who had been fortunate enough to find in his wife a moft amiable companion; but not being able to make a proper eftimation of his valuable prize, he neglected to pay her that tribute of refpect, which is due to merit of the firft quality. Like too many of the prefent age, he took a thought of acting the fafhionable gentleman, by keeping a courtezan, or concubine. To expoftulate with him upon the impropriety of his conduct, was but a vain attempt; for he

was

was too far gone in the difeafe called folly, to
recover all on a fudden. When juft ready to
fail, delufion had fo far repreffed the generous
feelings of affection, that a preference was given
to the dulcinea, by waiting firft upon her to receive her commiffion; which was extravagant
enough. The poor wife was confidered but as a
trifling piece of furniture, fcarce worth noticing:
however, in taking his leave, by way of irony,
he afked, if fhe had any particular demands? fhe
modeftly made him a reply, which I fancy he
did not expect, viz. that fhe would be quite
happy, and perfectly pleafed, if he only brought
her home a fhilling's worth of wifdom. After
reaching the place of his deftination, being fuccefsful in his voyage, and on the point of return-
ing home;—to the injunctions of the proftitute
he attended minutely; and the article wanted by
his wife was fo low priced, that he thought it
fhould alfo be fought for: And accordingly inquired at the firft convenient fhop, if they had
any wifdom to fell. But furprifed at the ftrange
queftion, he was kept in exercife, and directed
from one fhop to another, till he reached the
laft, which joined the quay; he entered it, with

afking

asking, as usual, if they sold a piece of finery, called Wisdom.

The merchant being a man of more than ordinary ingenuity, at once understood him, replied in the affirmative, and wished to know how much he wanted. But before I satisfy you in that singular demand, says he, permit me to ask you a few questions, and I hope you will answer them with candour: Who desired you to purchase this same wisdom? My wife. That tells me you are a bad boy, and that you do not treat her with that humanity, or generous attachment, that nuptial engagements would require, and that an honest heart, which has a sincere desire to live in harmony and happiness, has a just title to expect. I fear some base enchantress captivates your affection, and makes you neglect your wife. After awakening his surprise by a suggestion so unexpected, he honestly acknowledged the authenticity of his discovery.

I hope you will not be offended, then, though I should deliver my sentiments upon this subject with some degree of freedom. When a man or woman create misery to themselves, they ought, and do often, pay for their folly. No vice will

lose

lose its influence, till its deformity appears suf-
ficiently plain, to make us view it with aversion.
Delicacy of conduct suitable to the character of
a man, and a Christian, that will triumph over
whatever is hollow or unsound, is necessary to
be observed in an union which requires the
exercise of prudence, and permanency of affection. Treachery in marriage is a base merchan-
dize, that receives no sanction of approbation
from being so common in the world.

Those who break through the sacred restraint,
not only impose upon others, but also deceive
themselves. And while the substance of happiness flies much faster than their fancy can pur-
sue, like the roving cloud of a storm, there re-
maineth scarcely any shadow of comfort. You
are now going home; as soon as you get snug
into the harbour, land in your most shabby
dress; wait first on this same favourite, make
up a pitiful story of your losses and misfortunes, you will then see what reception you
meet with. Repair next to your wife, tell her
the same story, and you will effectually discern,
which of the two has the best claim to your

H   affection;

affection : for those who cease to love virtue, every good man, should ceafe to know.

He then took his leave, politely thanked him for his wifdom, and affured him he would clofe-ly adhere to his injunctions. The very day he reached his native shore, he forgot not to approach his miftrefs in the manner prescribed. His tattered drefs, or indigent appearance, was no great entertainment to her eyes; the difmal relation of his misfortunes, to her ears had no music. In short, inftead of expreffing the leaft feeling of fympathy for him, she immediately affumed her natural affurance, and bluntly told him, she was amazed how he had the impudence to come near her houfe; and charged him to shew her his face no more. He recovered at once from his former frenzy, and gave her to underftand, that he was certain her counfel would produce the defired effect, and that he was fully determined never to pay her another vifit. Then to his own habitation he haftily directed his willing fteps. His wife received him with a fmiling countenance, and a hearty welcome: before he had got half-way in his gloomy narration, with the fwelling tear

in

in her eye, she kindly interrupted him; and affured him, that it was not his money, but his
heart, she was anxious to fecure. Though she
had no defign to mix reproachful looks or language with her breathings of rejoicing; yet she
would make no fecret of her defire, nor attempt
to conceal her wish of fixing his affection. And
if in that point she could only be fuccefsful, she
would envy no one's happinefs. The merchant's
wifdom loft nothing of its value from importa-
tion. His heart was fenfibly touched with gratitude to the one for his valuable inftruction;
and with a glow of affection to the other, for
her unmerited attachment, which for fome moments could only be expreffed in the filent language of admiration. He then candidly revealed
the whole of the enigma, and from that day
ferioufly improved every opportunity of advan-
cing her happinefs: nor would he ever allow
any other woman to share in his heart, or divide
his love. Therefore I shall leave them in full
poffeffion of happinefs, and proceed to contemplate another picture.

Inconftancy always ranges without any fettled
object of defire; therefore, to fubdue this airy

spirit

spirit of novelty effectually, or change a taste
once accustomed to variety, is a task not easily
performed. Persons bred in the shades of retirement, instead of wandering among the meteors
of fashion, which dazzle the world by their elegance and novelty, would do well to consult
common sense: for to think of combining oppo-
site qualities, or form a coalition between dif-
positions, against which nature and habit have
declared perpetual enmity, is at once absurd and
impracticable. A writer of eminence is of o-
pinion, " That it would not be very difficult to
find a suitable companion, if every man was con-
tent with such as he is qualified to expect; but
if vanity tempts him to forsake his rank, and
post himself among those with whom no common
interest or mutual pleasure can ever unite him,
he must always live in a state of unsocial separa-
tion, without tenderness, and without trust."

Wherever an extravagant disparity of situa-
tions or education takes place, gratification,
though possible to be obtained, perhaps in some
particular cases, it would neither be safe nor
prudent to wish for, upon terms so unequal.
When happiness perches itself on an elevation
difficult

difficult to reach, and where all feeming freedom is facrificed in the acquifition, it would not
be amifs to make a fair calculation, early and
impartially, to view the object of purfuit, with
her mental and perfonal advantages, and to fee if
her qualities are fufficient to make a full compenfation for the anxiety they excite. The fable,
where the father fent his fon to the wood, with
inftructions, the firft day to cut as high as his
hand could reach, might dictate a leffon of wifdom, if wifdom could be caught from example.
When the tafk of the day was over, with the
tender feelings of fympathy, the father condoled
with him, as if he himfelf had fhared in the fatigue ; fo much indeed, that the young man was
afhamed to complain, although the effect of his
toil was fpeaking aloud, from every vein and
finew in his body. The next day's injunctions,
as much upon the other extreme, were, to cut as
clofe to the ground as poffible. When at night
he came home, attention and concern were ripe
for utterance, and the effufions of benevolence
were no lefs expreffive, than on the preceding
evening. The third and laft day, no arbitrary
meafures were prefcribed : The parent relieved

H 3   him

him from a taſk which he had hitherto performed with inconvenience and reluctance : A diſpen-
ſation was granted him, to take his mark oppo-
ſite to himſelf, without any particular order in
his operation. Finiſhing his taſk with a good
grace, he ſaunters home with the ſong of
triumph ; the father, however, ſeemed to take no
notice of his cheerfulneſs, but began to ſoothe
him, as formerly, with the ſalutation of tender-
neſs. Father, he replies, your particular concern claims my gratitude at all times ; but I
think it at this moment unneceſſary, for the
labour of this day looked more like play than
toil. My ſon, pauſe and reflect on what you
felt and ſaw, hearken not to me alone, but
rather to the voice of experience and wiſdom ;
for honour and advantage, reſult from their precepts.

Permit me to mention Miſs Lofty. Had a gratification of your taſte taken place, when much
againſt my pleaſure, your addreſſes were directed to her ; had you even reached the pinnacle
to which your views aſpired, perhaps you
would have found a gueſt altogether different,
and ſomething quite foreign from the happineſs
you

you had in expectation. You flew again to
Mifs Unfragrant: She, with equal arrogance,
might have given you the fauce of repentance,
or probably perpetual bondage would have been
the chains affigned you for life. The laft day
you was pleafed and happy, and feemed a perfect
mafter of your bufinefs; read from that plain
lecture, the part which you yourfelf ought to
act. Make choice of the female whofe education, tafte, feelings, devotion, and behaviour,
flow in a regular courfe; with whom you think
happinefs is in the greateft credit: for true tafte,
like Narciffus, is ftrongly taken with its own
likenefs. Lord Darnly, from his elegant appearance, rather than his merit, was raifed to
a rank far above what he had a right to afpire;
the duties of which he was incapable of dif-
charging, either with advantage to the kingdom,
or honour to himfelf. The unfortunate, but
accomplifhed Queen Mary, found to her coft,
when it was too late to complain, and when the
fallies of love, infpired by the impofition of external beauty, had loft their power to pleafe,
what ill-fkilled meffengers her eyes had been,
and the unfair report they had haftily made of
him

him with whom fhe was to lead her life; for to
this unequal choice all her fubfequent misfortunes might, with ftrong prefumption, be
afcribed.

A volume elegantly bound, if it contains little
information, neither fentiment, language, nor a
fupport of virtue, its external finery will foon
ceafe to pleafe, and its fair polifhed appearance,
which at firft excited commendation, will completely lofe its credit, and fuddenly fall into dif-
repute. Another, though not bound at all, if
it contains the marks of genuine refinement; if
every expreffion you perufe, and every page you
open, feem pregnant with the riches of merit,—
you are glad to fnatch—from the jaws of obfcurity, the remains of fo much beauty, and to
preferve it, though in a fhabby outward appearance, from the fate of abufe or decay.

The picture of marriage defcribed by a lively
imagination, or the gay colours of the Poet,
perhaps in romantic fcenery, may have more
of the fiction of a fable, than a delineation of
the real ftate; where all foreign deception
fhould be viewed with an eye of jealoufy, treated
as an enemy to which no ftation of credit fhould
be

be affigned. Many are ready to annex an idea
of finifhed felicity to matrimonial connection,—
confider it as the ferenity of a perpetual fun-fhine,
where no tempeftuous paffion rifes to ruffle the
mind; but a fenfible female will fhow her juft
opinion of the bufinefs, by the folidity of her reflections. She often confults the productions of
nature, for leffons of inftruction. She fees the
juvenile flower of the fpring, that makes fo fair
a fhew, and emits fuch a pleafant flavour, foon
ftript of all its gaudy colours, and its ftately
pride blafted in full blow. From pointing to a
figure fo tranfient in its nature, a difcouraging
difcuffion is not in the leaft intended. Though
it is too true, that many unhappy examples are
recorded in every age, and feen in every country,
notwithftanding of this, the facred engagement
fhould meet with no abufe from fuch an argument. When the torch of affection which leads
the party contracted to the bower of hymen, and
glows with mutual fincerity ; when it is before
hand underftood, as a connection where happinefs cannot be continued, without a particular
defire to render life agreeable to each other,—
the meaning, which never forfeits its natural
beauty

beauty or fenfe, has fhared in the relation.
And from a countenance fo fair, delight; in its
principal quality, may reafonably be expected.
When the prevailing tafte or hopes of happinefs,
fpring from the vain ideas of equipage and grandeur, and not from the good qualities of the
character propofed, it is eafy to imagine what
may be the confequence of meafures fo irregu-
lar and ill digefted. It is not in the palaces of
eaftern monarchs, that love without diffimulation has its feat of fame, or planet of dignity.
The mechanic of Indoftan may happily experience that periodical and fincere fatisfaction,
from the partner of his affection, which the
fovereign of a great nation, in the variety of his
enjoyments, and the confufion of his feraglio,
labours in vain to acquire. Sincerity and candour are the elements where virtue loves to
dwell, and happinefs to fmile: and where thefe
valuable companions are pleafed to refide, they
are fure to procure and continue affection, much
longer than wealth, grandeur, or Graham's cœ-
leftial bed. The Spectator is of opinion, that
fincerity and virtue are the firft articles to be
confulted; that where thefe fail on either fide,
enjoyment

enjoyment is feldom at home, and felicity at the beft but a fluctuating gueft. Challenges of fuperiority are laid afide, where real affection is underftood. Love is more than a fkilful mathematician; for he will eafily reconcile the lines of difference, and make them every where run parallel. Thofe who unite with a determined refolution of affection, of increafing their ftock, by fharing the pleafure or intereft of it equally with each other, will in a fhort time obtain that accumulation of téndernefs, which prevails only in the foil where goodnefs regulates the paffions. To the very filence of thofe we love, we generoufly afcribe ineffable charms : and the language of thofe we diflike, has a flaw in every expreffion ; all their periods feem rude and unedifying. When a profeffion of efteem is fraught with tendernefs, all the tranfactions of the day are conducted with good humour, and continued with frequent and ferious inftances of a happy underftanding. Where difaffection fpeaks no tone of victory ; where all its emotions are fuppreffed, before they fwell into a ftubborn difeafe, or habits of unhappy confequence,—pleafure and affection are then confined to their proper bounds.

For

For without the art of reafoning, it appears as
a plain fact, that if difguft once rifes into rage,
or violence, you may then look for the depar-
ture of peace, and hear her expiring voice pronounce a mournful farewell to the pleafures of
affection. Ah! what a difmal fcene! how dark
and cloudy the profpect! every trivial circumftance will carry the conftruction of a crime,
and even what is innocent in itfelf, to the eye of
diftruft has no beauty: comforts ficken into a
folitary fadnefs, or a raging ftorm; and in the
fpleen of difcontent, difcretion is effectually loft.
Therefore, to make the finews of affection durable, marriage requires that a fimilar tafte and
affection form every part of the agreement, and
continue to increafe in their progrefs through
the whole length of the relation. Thofe choice
characters, whofe minds are richly tinctured
with fenfibility, can never be at any great diftance from happinefs. While the brightening
beams of day fmile on their fteps, and join in
their company; when the fentiments and purfuits of this ftate are not feigned teftimonies,
but the folid and genuine fupport of mutual
endearment, pleafure then is fomething more
than

than an idle chimera, it is that glow of enthu-
siasm that elevates the generous votaries to the
first degree of rational delight. Therefore it
would be as great a wonder, to meet with clouds
of confusion in such a serene climate, as it
would to find diamonds in the barren hills of
Tenneriff. Before a marriage receives its date,
should the voice of correct understanding make
any inquiries, what may we suppose the qualifications that are mostly thought of, or considered as necessary to excite attention, and secure
esteem? The question might not be so much
framed to accord with the general practice, as
with the periods of a correct taste, and sage penetration. Is she very beautiful? has she many
courtiers? and what is her fortune? are not
the principal inquiries which should be made, or
with which a lasting prospect of felicity is na-
tively connected. It is not she who follows
slavishly the caprice of fashion, who is ready to
vary her taste, to suit the complexion of the times,
from whom the pleasures of contentment, or of
domestic enjoyments, may be expected. If much
information and learning, in the estimation of
some men, are not the qualities requisite to en-

courage-

courage happinefs, or form a pleafant female companion, I fhould think that ignorance could never make her more agreeable, nor more fit for a partner in life. The fong of the Ifraelitifh women, that Saul had killed but one thoufand, and David ten, is a plain proof, that, when a languid performance meets with a feeble encomium, meritorious actions ought to fhine.

The principal beauties that common fenfe fhould efteem, and for which it fhould make its demand, is a fenfible, feeling, and affectionate heart; a comely, modeft, and agreeable behaviour. Does religion infpire a young woman with that Chriftian charity, that will make her remain paffive or filent, and indicate no marks of rafh judgement or feverity, even when fhe cannot approve? Is it more from reality than fhew, that the witneffes of her piety fpeak plain and aloud? Thefe are refined qualifications; and if thefe are the friendly inftructions to be learned from her, happy, for ever happy, is he who fhall obtain her. He receives not all her portion at one payment; neither is it a yearly income; but, what is ftill better, a conftant and daily revenue. It is only where the joys of

freedom

freedom fhed their generous influence, that courtfhip is an act of inclination, or the effect of choice. During the force of the feudal fyftem, when the laws of chivalry were in vogue, ruffians or barbarians were often the moft fuccefsful in female conquefts ; but as fociety began to improve, and fighting became lefs fafhionable, the ridiculous exhibitions of a Don Quixotte began gradually to decline. Nothing can be more reafonable, than that love fhould direct in the choice of a partner for life ; and that the parties contracted in wedlock fhould enter into that compact with the moft genuine affection for each other. "Love," fays an eminent philofopher, " is a ftrong prefervative againft the infection of loofe example : it helps to fubdue all foreign oppofition in the way of refinement, and gives a neceffary fupply to the fineft virtues." To ftrengthen the foregoing affertion, I fhall relate an oral narration, where a fudden revolution of fentiments wrought wonders in a very fhort time. A recruiting officer, who, with his party, had been billeted in a certain town ; the firft night he was fo much engaged, that it was fomewhat late before he could make it convenient to go

home

home to his lodging; and in that cafe had not
an opportunity of feeing many of the family.
One of the daughters, with her companion, had
their room clofe to the one in which he lay.
After her firft fleep, recollecting fhe had forgot
to give the fervants fome inftructions neceffary
to be executed before morning, fhe rofe for that
purpofe, and foon difoharged the bufinefs; but
in her way backward, by miftake, went to the
captain's apartment, in place of her own. She lay
by him for fome time, without the leaft fufpicion of having changed her companion; but hap-
pening to reach her hand over his breaft, fhe
difcovered her error, and, as much afraid as fhe
was furprifed, immediately leapt out of bed;
but he awakening, was equally alert, and in a
moment fecurely locked her in his arms.
Finding he was determined not to part with her
eafily, fhe addreffed him with the utmoft civility.
My good Sir, I prefume, from your profeffion,
that you are a man of honour, and would not
wifh to expofe a miftaken female to unmerited
ridicule. I am under a contract of marriage,
and my fate is to be decided by twelve to-morrow:
Therefore, in cafe you do not defift, I fhall cer-
tainly

tainly alarm the whole family. Well, fays he, fince fuch is the cafe, I fhall comply with your requeft, on condition that you promife to make me your beft man. She at once agreed to the propofal, obtained her liberty, and concealed her danger.

In the morning, upon his being introduced to the bride, fhe effectually fhook his military bravery. Mr Love, that cunning engineer, immediately brought all his artillery to play, and laid a clofe fiege to his heart. He was altogether charmed with her appearance, and her great good fenfe was equally captivating. He faw that no time was to be loft; therefore, like a fkilful artificer, began his counter work, and confidered all advantages as fair. The clergyman, when the party appeared, fuppofed all objections removed, and was proceeding to unite them, when the officer thus addreffed her intended hufband: You may think yourfelf at liberty to marry her, but I declare upon honour fhe was in bed with me laft night. She blufhed from ear to ear, and the whole family was in confufion. The bridegroom, without any inquiry into this myfterious bufinefs, takes his hat, and

fwears

fwears fhe fhould never bed with him. Having
been fo far fortunate in getting rid of the chief
metropolitan, he fteps forward with thefe words:
If my hand can be any compenfation for what
you have loft, it is quite ready for your reception. After a ferious converfation on the fubject,
giving a minute detail of all the circumftances,
and the caufe that gave rife to his declaration,
fhe learned the beauties of his character, accept-
ed of his offer, and with mutual confent, they
were inftantly united. The fenfible thoughts
of the comedian are, in this fingular cafe, fomewhat applicable: " O marriage! happieft,
eafieft, fafeft ftate ; let debauchees and drunkards,
fcorn thy rights, how can the favage call it lofs
of freedom, thus to converfe with, thus to gaze
at, a faithful, beauteous friend: Blufh not, my
fair one, that my love applauds thee; nor be it
painful to be my wedded wife, that my full
heart o'erflows in praife of thee. Thou art by
law, by intereft, and by paffion mine: Paffion and
reafon join in love of thee." And I take it for
granted, that they lived quite happy, as I never
heard the leaft rumour tranfpire to the contrary.

To

To fpeak in the ftyle of common fenfe, away
with what the world calls a pretty fellow, or a
handfome female; let me have honour, and the
continued virtues which regularly flow from a
good heart;—thefe are the foundation on which
matrimonial felicity can be erected, and erected
with fecurity.

Where thefe take root, affection will remain
much longer than the honey month: love will
not cloy with wedlock, nor lofe its falutary influence by a nearer acquaintance. Mr Thom-
fon, in his finifhed picture of hymeneal happinefs,
alike difplays the ingenuity of the moralift, the
painter, and the poet: -

> " O happy they! the happieft of their kind,
> Whom gentler ftars unite, and in one fate
> Their hearts, their fortunes, and their beings blend.
> 'Tis not the coarfer tie of human laws,
> Unnatural oft, and foreign to the mind,
> That binds their peace; but harmony itfelf,
> Attuning all their paffions into love;
> Where friendfhip full exerts her fofteft power,
> Perfect efteem, enlivened by defire
> Ineffable, and fympathy of foul.
> Thought meeting thought, and will preventing will,
> With boundlefs confidence; For nought but love

Can

Can anſwer love, and render bliſs ſecure,
Let eaſtern tyrants, from the light of heaven
Seclude their boſom ſlaves, meanly poſſeſs'd
Of a mere lifeleſs, violated form :
While thoſe whom love cements in holy faith,
And equal tranſport, free as nature live,
Diſdaining fear. What is the world to them,
Its pomp, its pleaſure, and its nonſenſe all !
Who in each other claſp whatever fair
High fancy forms, and laviſh hearts can wiſh,
Truth, goodneſs, honour, harmony, and love,
The richeſt bounty of indulgent Heaven."

SPRING, p. 69 & 70.

The moraliſt obſerves, that only one ſort of love
is to be found, although he allows a thouſand
different copies of it. As a ſpecimen of the firſt
quality, a very affecting anecdote is related of a
young woman in France, " who, after many dif-
ficulties, at laſt obtained her parents conſent of
marrying one ſhe ſincerely loved ; but being to
ſign the inſtrument of contract, ſhe had no ſoon-
er written the firſt letter of her name, than with
the exceſs of joy, ſhe fell into a fainting fit,
from which ſhe could never be recalled to life."
What a valuable prize muſt her lover have loſt !
and to him in particular, what a cloud of ſorrow
her death would occaſion ! Goodneſs of heart,
richly

richly adòrned with the delicate feelings of affection, inchants all who perceive it, and well deferves to be ftyled the flower of beauty, which
the pencil of the beft artift cannot eafily imitate,
and but rarely, in its juft features, exprefs the
original. Thofe eminently poffeffed of it, fpeak
with their eyes, and being filent fubdue.

To meet with a perfon qualified in the various
fignifications of the word, to bear the facred character of a friend, is a difcovery not more rare
than divine. Demofthenes called impofition in
love, the witchcraft of affection. Leonado da
Vinci, an Italian painter, was of opinion, that
fome fublime fubjects are beft defcribed by negatives. Therefore he gives a delineation of falfe
friendfhip, by an ivy thrufting down the wall on
which it grew. Examples may eafily be multiplied, in every age and country, to preferve
the credit of this painter's negatives. But the
genuine is not fo eafily defaced; like the good
tree, it will prove its quality by the character
of its fruit. The wintry blaft of oppofition will
not obfcure its fame, nor retard its progrefs.
Perhaps the following relation may not be altogether out of feafon, it is a copy of fingular benevolence.

nevolence. I muſt own I think the introduction
highly over-ſtrained, and a ſacrifice to which
very few, influenced by real affection, would ever
have conſented. But if the prologue is ſome-
what inconſiſtent, the cataſtrophe produces every
event neceſſary to form as fine a picture of ſincere affection, as ever was exhibited in dramatic
dreſs. A young Roman repaired to Athens, to
finiſh his education, reputed at that time one of
the firſt ſeminaries of inſtruction, in that or any
other country. Fate, which often acts with ir-
reſiſtible authority, and has a ſurpriſing power
in forming connections, preſented him, in a
ſhort time, with a companion deſerving of his
eſteem, in the moſt extenſive latitude. They ſoon
became a principal topic of converſation ; every
eye beheld them with wonder, every tongue was
laviſh in their praiſe. As a phenomenon of this
nature has commonly ſomething in its progreſs
out of the uſual mode, we ſhall haſten to view
the ſingular traits of this friendly painting.
The Athenian had fixed his eyes on a female of
merit and family. The partiality with which
ſhe was diſtinguiſhed by virtue ſo conſpicuous,
and a character adorned with the firſt-rate abilities,

ties, as well as a combination of all the other
beauties requisite to speak a polished mind, could
not but be flattering : so that the increase of her
affection kept pace with his own : so soon as
the secret took wing, it was wafted abroad ;
conversation caught the report, and accelerated
its progress, in proportion to the prevailing element of affection or humour through which it
passed. Circumstances were so favourably conducted, that all their acquaintances unanimously
concluded their happiness sure, and fast ripening
into enjoyment ; when a new event hastily
started up, to change its direction, and to damp
the joy of this so much wished for felicity.
The Roman was all of a sudden seized with a
complication of maladies, which seemed to prog-
nosticate at least a raging fever, if not a more
fatal consequence. Physicians were called, me-
dicines applied, and proper nurses provided ; but
his complaint seemed to have taken so firm a
root, as to baffle the power of every application.
The Athenian, who felt more on the occasion
than the whole of his acquaintances, and who
was scarcely a moment from his side, seeing
him one day somewhat calm, and none but themselves

felves in the room, he turned the converfation
to the fymptoms of his diforder, and hinted that
he thought them more of a mental, than of a
bodily nature. He candidly replied, that the
caufe of his ficknefs ought to remain for ever a
fecret, as he knew the cure would not be obtained. He was of opinion, in a fituation fo
critical, that concealment was neceffary, and
common prudence required it. My aftonifhment
is great, and the found I can fcarcely credit:
What! fays the Grecian, has our friendfhip
all along been a bubble? What have you ever
feen in my conduct to give the leaft authority
to all this diftruft? Is my fincere attachment
treated with the ungenerous conftruction of
hatred? No facrifice would I grudge, however
coftly, that could be the happy means of purchafing confolation, or of reftoring your health.
Paufing for a reply, after giving vent to a group
of broken fighs, the expreffion ftole from the
Roman, as if expiring for want of confidence
to utter it. " Your female friend," was all that
his faultering tongue could pronounce. He
looked at him, and feemed to be loft in filent
tendernefs; but after an apparent ftruggle with
his

his feelings, he thus spoke: Kind fate, direct me
in this critical dilemma, both how to speak and
act. If I gratify my own inclination, I lose my
friend: If I relinquish her to whom I have
already offered my hand, my honour shall be
tarnished with a cloud of disgrace, and my name
branded with lasting infamy: Well, let the
world justify my conduct, or condemn me: let
it say what it will, I am resolved to prolong your
life; live, and she shall surely be yours. The
preliminaries are already adjusted, and the day
of our marriage is fixed. A proposal from you,
at so late a period, might in reality be deemed
an insult; and your hopes of happiness prove
precarious, perhaps be for ever frustrated. I
will marry, and you shall bed with her. Into
her apartment I will convey you privately, and
when the light is extinguished, return, and leave
you to occupy my place; in hopes that Providence may so regulate matters, as that our rash
enterprise may at least terminate in your happiness, whatever frowns of fortune I may have
yet to encounter. The promise was made with
sincerity, and the engagement immediately performed. The light of the morning made a dif-

K   covery,

covery, not more new than unexpected. Her
amazement was so great, that she could scarcely
credit her own eyes; to make an apology, or
proposals of reconciliation, was but labour in
vain. She soon left him to ruminate on the rash
part he had acted; and went to consult her
parents, how to regulate herself, and what she
should resolve on. After the first gust of passion
was in some measure subdued, and reason began
to resume its empire, they, as well as herself,
thought it the best policy to wink at, or at least
appear passive in respect of all that had passed;
and, as the next creditable step, agreed that they
should also be married. A train so favourable,
unlocked the Athenian, and made him venture
once more to show them his face. Rather out
of compliment to the Roman, than any regard
they had for himself, they seemed to treat him
with their usual politeness; and in appearance
he shared as formerly in their kindness. But so
soon as the married couple departed, and went
home to Rome, he felt the effect of their resent-
ment: her relations could no longer conceal their
spleen; a confiscation of all his property immediately took place. His name was erased from

their

their public records; and they paſſed a decree, in which he was baniſhed for ever from the city. Not knowing where to direct his ſteps, he wandered from place to place, till his dreſs had almoſt loſt its colour, as well as his character its credit. One day muſing on paſt tranſactions, all at once he awakens from his dream of uncertain peregrination. Was it for nothing I made a conqueſt of my affection? Shall not he for whom I loſt my all, meet me with the face of a friend? let me at leaſt make a trial.—His courage ſupported him very well on his journey, till he reached the ſuburbs of the city; but the moment he entered Rome, and underſtood the rank and dignity to which his friend was raiſed, reflections on his own miſconduct ſtared him in the face, and damped the ardour of his reſolution. The eye of him who had beheld his better days, and ſeen him baſking in the ſun-ſhine of fortune, he could not bear to encounter in the weeds of a pilgrim. Entertaining no concern from the danger of wild beaſts, or the fear of famine, he formed a haſty reſolution, of retiring to the woods, and concealing himſelf from the eye of the world; for life was already become a burden.

K 2 .   He

He only proceeded a fhort way, when he was
violently affailed with furious winds and rain ;
but kind Providence had not yet deferted him :
a hofpitable cove appeared in view, which feemed
to encourage and invite him to take fhelter under
its generous roof. Fatigue and anxiety foon
drew the curtain of repofe over his weary eye-
lids; and that reft, which often forfakes the
bed of down, lent him its falutary enjoyment,
in his folitary habitation.

The brightening beams of day had fcarcely
begun to fmile, when the echo of an alarm re-
founded from every corner of his lonely grotto.
The fteps of the traveller had been haftily interrupted by the view of a mangled body, which
had fallen a victim to the favage hand of fome
degenerate heart. Sufpecting, from his appearance and fituation, this barbarous action to be
the confequence of his lawlefs exertion, he is
charged with the horrid murder, and has nothing
to offer in his own defence. No oppofition being
given, he is thought to have freely acknowledged
himfelf the perpetrator of this cruel act, and con-
fequently foon lodged in a fituation, deftined to
contain characters of coarfer feelings, and of
much

much more depraved morals, than his own.
When he was brought before the judges, however, he was foon recognifed by one of them;
his former friend who plainly perceived ftrong
traces of his old companion in his countenance,
afked his name, and if ever he had been at
Athens. He anfwered in the affirmative. The
judge, without any further ceremony, threw off
his gown, placed himfelf clofe by his fide, and
declared himfelf the delinquent. A ferious altercation took place, and the contention was
maintained with determined firmnefs. The
whole court, quite aftonifhed, appointed them
different apartments, till fome inquiry fhould be
made into this dark chapter of accidents. Remorfe feized the real criminal, when the noife of
this fingular relation reached his ear; and even
though at a diftance from the feat of juftice, he
appears there upon the next day of trial. Each
of the other two ftill adhered to the point they
had formerly advanced. But this third perfon
places the cafe in a quite different pofition; as
well as in colours much more natural. The
candid ftrain of his addrefs foon commanded
attention, while he thus fpoke: Thefe men can

K 3   in

in no form come under the defcription of agref-
fors. He then fincerely wifhed the fame tone
of juftification could be applied to himfelf. But
he would by no means attempt to extenuate
either his difgrace, or his guilt. He declared
that he could not endure the thought, that two
innocent perfons fhould fuffer either accufation,
or punifhment, for what he alone had committed.
He then acknowledged the atrocioufnefs of his
crime, and that it was at variance with the laws
of God, contrary to every feeling of humanity;
and that all fuch criminals were not only a reproach to the name of man, a difhonour to their
relations and country, but were alfo left a prey
to endlefs mifery. He ftill further obferved,
that the inteftine wars occafioned by fuch out-
rageous breaches of juftice, and the facred obligations which are the bond of union in all civilized nations, or well regulated focieties, was
always followed by an incurable difeafe. Therefore, without the leaft equivocation, he would
fettle the gloomy bufinefs before them, by the
only amendment then in his power, which was
a free confeffion of his guilt, and a facrifice of
himfelf to juftice. His criminal conduct deferved

ved the feverest punishment, and he felt a remorse
much more poignant than any one elfe could
paint or defcribe. Whatever degree of feverity
the judges, in their wifdom, might fee proper
to inflict, he would ftrive to bear with becoming
refignation; a duty which is laudable, when
confcience fupports the mind, and pleads freedom
from the charge of depravity; but nowife meritorious when loaded with accumulated accu-
fations of guilt. The generous open manner of
the offender excited univerfal compaffion; he
foon felt the effect of their clemency, for the
prevailing voice cried for a pardon; which was
granted without hefitation. The innocence of
the other two being fufficiently teftiffed, they
were difmiffed with a degree of aftonifhment,
bordering on veneration. The judge takes his
friend into a private family, where they were at
liberty to enjoy themfelves. He infifted on a
true relation of all his misfortunes, fince the
time of their feparation: and fo foon as he
finifhed his narration, faid to him, My good
friend, how much am I indebted to you? and
how much do I ftill owe you? I fhall lay all
ceremony afide, and fhow that I am not quite
ungrateful.

ungrateful. I have a fifter, whom I will venture to recommend as a wife. Should her perfon
and manner gratify your tafte, I promife that
every other confideration fhall be made agreeable
to you ; for you fhall fhare in my fortune and
friendfhip, while I live. This Roman female
poffeffed extraordinary merit ; and, upon the
whole, it was thought he had gained much
by the exchange. Their remaining days were
uncommonly fortunate, and continued to fhine
with the rays of unbroken felicity.

The opinion of thofe diftinguifhed by tafte
and difcernment, refpecting women as well as
other objects, will always bear refleftion.
Though every found deferves not to be fet to
mufic, the following fenfible quotation requires
no apology : " A female of merit, whofe mind is
improved by a virtuous and refined education,
retains, in her declining years, an influence over
the men more effectual, than ever fhe acquired
by her beauty : fhe is then the delight of her
friends, as much as fhe was formerly that of
her admirers : for a refpectable character is a
flower which we cultivate for its fcent or beauty,
one of the graces of nature, one of the objects
which

which beautify the creation, admired by all
men in all ages, which our fathers valued, and
which we after them likewife efteem." How
ftately does female elegance appear, when it
comes forward adorned with the rich colours,
neat attire, and polifhed ftrokes of the hiftorian;
or, when defcribed by the no lefs expreffive
pencil, and beautiful delineations of the poet.
The united efforts of thefe painters give fuch a
glow of animation to the whole picture, as to
make the reader almoft wifh for a fight of the
original character: What a beautiful encomium,
how fimple, unaffected, and laconic, is that
which was made on Phocion's wife: " She firft
arrayed herfelf in meeknefs and temperance, and
then put on whatever more was neceffary."
The character of Pliny's wife is likewife com-
prehenfive, and briefly expreffed; who was faid
to be " the beft of wives, and the beft beloved."
The reprefentation is natural, eafy, and divine.
The idea thefe convey will require no dictiona-
ry to explain; the conftruction is quite obvious.
Sincerity of heart, and fimplicity of outward
appearance, are the ornamental habit of her who
deferves to be taken notice of. " Solomon, who
had

had made the tour of the fashionable world, complains, (Ecclef. vii. 28.), "that one man among a thousand he had found, but a woman in all that number he found not." I suspect much, when he uttered this harsh expression, he had been too often conversant with women of inferior worth, and therefore seldom met with any heroine of sterling merit, who loved virtue too sincerely, to sacrifice it for a shadow; and admired a good name more than his dazzling grandeur. Were he to appear in our age, how much would he seem surprised, to find many of our females so far superior to those of his time. The treasure of genuine virtue, and the flow of disinterested benevolence, is not the production of every soil, nor the principal feature of every character; but I know one whose life and manners brighten to the view, like the cheerful smiling sun, whose merit requires no panegyric; who is singular in every moral virtue; whose heart will melt with tenderness, and shed the tear of sympathy for sorrows not her own; whose silent sense and modesty utter a thousand beauties; whose very looks are expressive of purity. I could name her, who,

when

when others were folded in the arms of fleep, or
fpending their morning-hours in adjufting their
drefs, and trifling away time at their toilet, —
has been diligently engaged in a different em-
ployment, and has been ready to fhare with
others the fruit of her labour; liberally fup-
plying the poor, and reaching her bread to the
needy. Models of this kind have been found in
palaces, and examples worthy of imitation fen
in a cottage; fo that we can neither fix on rank
in life as the ftandard of excellence, nor look
for genuine goodnefs for ever in low ftations.
A plebeianefs, who, under many difadvantages,
fhould maintain elegance in her manner, judgement in her tafte, and virtue in all her actions,
would furely deferve to be faluted as the morning ftar; and no good heart would ever envy
her fuccefs in the world, however eminent the
ftation to which fhe might be raifed. Sem-
pronia had been much diftinguifhed by the liberal gifts of fortune, befides high birth, genteel
education, and engaging wit; fhe was alfo in
poffeffion of (what the giddy and thoughtlefs
would value more than the generous endowments
of modefty), incomparable beauty: yet thefe
were

were no fcreen of protection, when the gloomy
meffenger of terror arofe in hafte to falute her.
Why heaves her breaft? what robs her of her
gaiety? When languifhing on a death-bed, does
fhe read with joy each day's fucceffive improvement? Does her fun look bright at its fetting?
Is the curtain every where embellifhed with the
pleafing beams, in which former years were
clad? Does the part fhe has acted exhibit the
reprefentation of a rich landfcape, under loaded
increafe in every direction, and fweetly perfumed with fragrant flowers? Ah! behold her
looking back with a blufhing countenance on the
falfe evanefcent fcene! when the tide of vice ran
high, when depravity rufhed on with impetuo-
fity, and vanity rolled on vanity. See the gloomy
fpectre of awakened crimes, angry, fulky, ftalk-
ing in fad and fable robes! What may we fuppofe the tone of her thoughts, at the clofing period of life? "Happy thofe who fed their minds
with Virtue's confcious dignity." Nearer the ap-
parition then approaches, reaves from her the
hopes of future fame, and gives the deadly blow.
How different the colours of life, in the character of the virtuous female, and her who has

ı   fled

fied from decency. What a degree of fincere
affection, and moral refinement will naturally
command, when nicely connected with the beauties of virtue. What an affecting picture do we
fee in the defcription of Virginia: her tragical
conclufion in the caufe of virtue, one would
imagine, might foften even the heart of a favage; and draw tears from eyes unaccuftomed to
weep. What feeling heart, in poffeffion of the
leaft fpark of humanity, could behold, unmoved,
an innocent female, in the blooming graces of
youth, ftruggling to preferve her honour un-
fullied, defpifing the wealth and power of a
Decemvir, while her virtue and fame were in
jeopardy!

This angel-form, though ever loaded with a
burden of forrow, appears with furprifing dignity. Her beams were heavenly, and might
have been expected to fhine long, with unclouded
ed luftre; but, ah! how dark and gloomy the
fcene is become! See her fair bofom fwelling
with killing and unmerited pain. That innocence that needs not fear any eye, nor dread the
glare of day; that great guardian of virtue, in
this difgraceful cafe, finds neither credit nor

L   compaffion.

compaffion. Like a menial flave, this treafure
of virtue, is led to the forum. There the un-
righteous judge had already appeared, and what
was to be expected from a wretch who had laid
his confcience afleep, and, as a flave to infamy,
had already devoted this unfortunate maid to
ruin. Who could behold her in fuch imminent
danger, and remain callous? Who could look
at her face, and obferve her eye overflow with
the tears of diftrefs, like rolling waves chacing
each other, where formerly pure affection darted
its enlivening beam,—and not fincerely regret
the transformation of the fcene? " The glowing
fympathy that feels, and kindly fpeaks the accents of the heart," could not but fhare in her
fufferings, and forely lament to fee virtue fo
confpicuous fo cruelly oppreffed. But as the
infamous name of Appius muft excite univerfal
abhorrence, to dwell longer on this uncommon
cataftrophe, can be no pleafant tafk to any
perfon tinctured with the leaft colour of humanity.

Having no particular characters in view in
thefe delineations, and no other defign than to
reprefent the diftinction which genuine virtue

ought

ought to introduce, inſtead of pretending to a
correſponding key, or looking for a character to
whom the imputation may belong, it is beſt, in
every caſe, to take care not to deſerve the firſt,
and pray to God, that a copy of the laſt may
not be ſeen in our days, nor ever acted in our
land.

"A good name," ſays the great King of Iſrael,
"is better than precious ointment." The voice of
fame ſurely deſerves reſpect, and ſolid judgement will always think ſo. Regularity of conduct, or conſiſtency of ſentiment, can ſeldom
ariſe, and will never continue long on a falſe
foundation: neither ſhall deceiving colours maintain the credit of reality for any length of time.
Envy, with low deſigns, too often finds a ſecret
pleaſure in eclipſing the luſtre it cannot reach;
but however artfully the dagger of detraction
may be directed, it will generally miſs its aim,
if truth forms no part of the accuſation. In
the ſober breaſt, juſtice erects its throne, where,
next to the approbation of an all-ſeeing eye,
conſcience occupies the character of a judge.
In vain ſhall the world acquit, when criminality
is the reſult of its deciſion; and if the inward

L 2

monitor

monitor freely abfolve, the falfe fentence which
the tongue of malice may uncharitably pafs,
ought to fit very eafy. On the female of character
many gaze, not with a defign to copy her elegance, but to fearch for imperfections : and the
fewer of thefe they difcover, the more fecure
will her beauty remain; but the greater is their
difappointment. Mankind, in a body, are not
eafily impofed upon; and the fame which difcretion, or an amiable line of conduct, never fails
to eftablifh, will always bear an infpection, and
always continue in eftimation. But the female
who confiders the public opinion as a matter
of fpeculation or indifference, muft have departed a great way from the path of common fenfe.
A pane of glafs, when once broken, can never
be cemented, fo as not to offend the eye, or
efcape difcernment. It is much better to wear
a meagre name, than an wounded virtue. Should
a character have the misfortune to fuffer from
falfe afperfions, while innocence remains un-
fhaken, it will foon have its refurrection and
credit; fpring up, with unwithered bloom, in
its genuine vigour; and when once the reproachful clouds are fcattered, its luftre, inftead

of

of fading from an unmerited eclipfe, will rather reach the meridian of beauty. " One hour changed the fetters of Jofeph into a chain of gold ; and he was honoured with the fecond chariot in Egypt !" Good offices torment malice, much more than any other kind of revenge : for when ill-defigned perfons are once able to throw their opponent off the hinges of difcretion, then they are quite in their element, let tart words fall, and fet inquiry at work ; but by bearing the ftorm patiently, the arrows of premeditated ruin will at laft recoil on thofe who difcharged them, without any injury to the perfon againft whom they were directed. Having flipped away rather abruptly from the allufion to the pane of glafs, I fhall here give it another glance. The female character is equally delicate, and liable, when a flaw is vifible, to the fame rules of criticifm : like the bite of the tarantula, it can never be cured. Therefore fterling reputation is truly no fmall ornament. Men of the moft diffipated morals cannot always fupport their own theory, at the expence of goodnefs ; nor refufe their fecret tribute of refpect to the female of finifhed qualifications ; nor is

the

the heart of any fo wicked, as to confider virtue
in reality as a piece of ufelefs furniture ; however much in their own vicious practice they
may affect to defpife it. The amiable female,
who has given ftrong and repeated proofs of a
correct tafte, and a fteady uniformity of morals,
who blufhes not at the unfafhionable epithets of
piety and religion, nor is afhamed to be ranked
in the antiquated number of thofe who will not
lay afide fuch ornaments, for the fneer of ridicule,
or the laugh of the profligate, carries in her
poffeffion a face of durable beauty, and a fhield
of invincible fecurity.

How ungenerous to reproach a female, when
we ought to admire her virtues. But it is a
felf-evident truth, that uncommon difcretion, or
beauty of mind, is an open infult to inferior or
hypocritical characters. When thofe who have
undervalued themfelves by impropriety of conduct, view the competition as beyond their
reach, and plainly obferve, that their own name
and fame cannot procure them the fame refpect,
nor rife to the fame ftandard of excellence.
The confequence is, that they contemplate the
female of merit, with the fpiteful eye of envy;

and

and that only for poffeffing advantages which
feem to place their own folly fo much in view.
Therefore, they feldom fail to watch narrowly,
and if they find the leaft flaw, they foon pefter
the world with the publication of it ; and the
fruit of their induftry is ufually attended with
large commentary notès, calculated either to
divert the attention of others from the inconfi-
ftency of their own conduct, or, if poffible, to
reduce a model of diftinguifhed qualities to the
fame level with themfelves. But thefe are glaring frailties, which carry in their train a ftrong
tincture of fpleen, without the leaft mixture of
charity, emulation, or refinement. To the female defirous of fupporting a fair reputation,
difcretion would dictate to fee fuch but feldom,
and neither to covet their fpirit, nor excite their
malice. Thofe who intereft themfelves in failings,
for which they are not to anfwer, tarnifh the
luftre of that humanity to which they might lay
claim, if felf-diffidence was a little more natural
to them. Many, in delineating the character of
their acquaintances, give the picture all the dark
colours of revenge, without a fingle fhade of
compaffion, or Chriftian charity. The reflection,
. . that

that probably they may have greater infirmities of their own to rectify, is removed from their recollection, as a thought they do not chuse to entertain. But it would not be amiss for those who are influenced by this humour, to confider, at the time when they are wantonly circulating their invectives, very likely on innocence, that by fuch unpolite, inelegant defcriptions, the complexion of their own hearts is lefs or more expofed to view. If thofe who are fo very fond of cenfure could be perfuaded to dwell more at home, probably the faults of others would not entertain them fo highly : for if we expect the fcreen of clemency, as a covering to our own imperfections, it is neceffary to look with an eye of fympathy on thofe of others. Thefe leffons of benevolence, if well learned, and regularly digefted, are all calculated to promote refpect, and procure happinefs. The female of difcretion will know all this; and therefore, if the failings of her acquaintances come under the eye of her infpection, fhe will make them a copy of inftruction to refine upon, and not a fubject of criticifm to declaim againft. She fhows herfelf the Chriftian by her language, as well as by her practice.

practice. She raifes herfelf to refpect; but it is by humanity and virtue, not by depreciating the character of others. In every circle, a female, on her firft appearance, has her accomplifhments called in queftion; her merit haftily, and often uncandidly decided; proportionable to the tafte or difpofition of the party, or the illiberal fentiments of the rafh critic, who afpires at the privilege of a judge, and paffes fentence with a tone of affurance, equal to the Grand Seignior, or as if he himfelf were abfolutely perfect. Even in this age of refinement, every female, defirous to maintain an unblemifhed character, will find that caution is not become an obfolete term, but is fully as neceffary now as it was in preceding periods. A modeft engaging manner, a meek humane heart, in connection with a ripe underftanding, though the richeft of jewels, (experience may convince us), do not always prove that rock of fecurity, or lafting refuge, that ignorance of mankind, or of the world, feem ready or willing to admit. Ungenerous criticifms too often borrow their authority from deliberate mifchief, and extend their fatal influence with the cruelty of favages. This dangerous

gerous fpirit, or poverty of morals, is not found
in the volume of charity,—but in the book of ill-
nature; and, according to its Pagan text, human
nature is at times examined, not with any grains
of allowance for the imperfections incident to
mortals, but rather as if they ought to poffefs
the perfection of angels. Should a female regulate her conduct by the rules of referve, feem
diftant and cautious, the epithet prude is liberally beftowed on her; if fhe is agreeable, open,
and unaffected, the imputation of levity is pro-
nounced, with equal impropriety. It were to be
wifhed, this cenforious fafhion would effectually
ceafe, and that proper encouragement were given
to habits of plain honefty.

I fhall fuppofe the fcene of action, for the following narration, in the ifland of Man; but whether it is merely an ideal picture, or the materials of real occurrences, conducted by the irrefiftible authority of a divine hand, I will by no
means take upon me to determine. Pofitively
to fix the fignature of Truth, to actions related
in the ftyle of romance, would be highly improper, and far from treating that venerable figure
with the refpect due to its dignity. Though I

do

do not recollect to have found any traces of the
following story, in either hiftory or novels, yet
I muſt acknowledge I have heard ſomething that
bore a ſtrong reſemblance to the principal characters; but if its phyſiognomy has not undergone
a complete repair, it has at leaſt the credit of a
modern dreſs. Allowing it to be nothing elſe
but the child of fancy, pernicious conſequences
cannot poſſibly enſue from a deſire of refining on
mental beauty: for if the moral it inculcates
reflects the leaſt credit on the intereſt of virtue,
or gives vice that degrading aſpect which tends
to produce diſtaſte, and prevent imitation, the
painting cannot be detrimental to either law or
goſpel.

Peel is one of the towns in Man. And what
though we ſhould make Mr Griffin one of the
principal characters in this relation, with an
eſtate well cultivated, and free from all incum-
brances. And what if we ſhould alſo ſuppoſe
the old man, his father, lingering on a death-bed,
and quite emaciated, calling his only ſon before
him to receive his laſt bleſſing and counſel, and
addreſſing him in a ſtrain ſimilar to the following:
" My ſon, liſten to the voice of inſtruction. Did
you

you ever hear an orator treat his fubject in a
more pathetic ftyle, than the expreffive eloquence
of agitation, ficknefs, and death? The end of all
motion is reft: the end of life is death. The
fun rejoiceth in his progrefs, and fo does man in
his ftrength; but his ftrength continueth not.
He flourifhes for a while, and then vanifheth for
ever.   Eternity is a pleafing profpect; but
what makes it fo? only the reflection of a well-
fpent life.   Therefore, my fon, if you wifh to
triumph over the fear of diffolution, and to be
put in poffeffion of invariable happinefs, at the
clofe of that important period, let fincerity
direct your devotion, and conftant attention to
equity characterife your actions; let love to
God, and benevolence to men, comprehend the
fignification, and exemplify your belief of the
foundeft articles of Chriftian faith.   To fly in
the face of every facred obligation, is impiety
in its moft glaring colours; and exultation in
fuch conduct exhibits a picture too dark to deferve approbation: a picture which few could
have the infolence to recommend.   Thofe who
give fugitive fhadows the place of folid fubftan-
ces, or vaguely imagine that the refufe of their
days,

days, or the dregs of their years, is a fit offer-
ing for their Maker, make an exceedingly unjuft calculation of the bufinefs. The beautiful
colours, and engaging features, of him who is
ripe in divine improvement, is a mark of diftinction worthy of unfading laurels ; and which
can fcarcely be heightened, unlefs it be by a con-
traft with him who is grown old in fin. Agreeable to the fyftem of learned fages, an honeft
man (while oftentation is fuppreffed) will gain
more by letting the world fee him as he is, than
by ftriving to appear what he is not. Boafting
is always thought to proceed from ignorance of
the world, and on that account is confidered as
a defect in politenefs. Xenophòn fays, that
praifes have a very mufical and charming accent
from the mouth of another, but are very flat and
untunable when they terminate in felf-exalta-
tion. Profit or pleafure is the ruling principle,
or animating power of all our purfuits. We
all know, that whatever is leaft attended with
feelings of remorfe, or grounds of repentance,
muft claim the clofeft connection with happinefs :
a command of temper, united with virtue and
integrity, poffeffes this inherent quality, and

M

therefore

therefore the cultivation of it is not only commendable, but abfolutely neceffary. Pyrrhus, a
famous fencing-mafter, " when any fcholar came
to learn his art, propofed, for the firft leffon, to
fubdue himfelf; for Anger, he obferved,
would look where to ftrike, but not where to
defend." Among other judicious inftructions,
we may naturally fuppofe, that the matrimonial
connection would be recommended, and the character of the female from whom the greateft
fhare of happinefs might be expected defcribed.
Tafte bears a fignificant emphafis, and ought to
be the predominant principle in an engagement
of fo much importance. Both the heart and eye
fhould have fair play; becaufe a gratification
from any other confideration than that of fincere
affection, can afford only a precarious profpect
of happinefs; for forced love can produce no
pleafing effect. The fame fincerity that directs
the tongue of candor to fpeak kind language,
will engage the heart of humanity to gratify
the hopes it has raifed. The fcriptures ftrongly
recommend to follow peace with all the world.
The mode in which you may beft acquit yourfelf, in the different relations of life, is clearly
and

and beautifully delineated in the expreſſive pages of inſpiration. And the divine oracles are by far the beſt commentary you can conſult, in regard to your duty. ' My ſon, this is all I am able to ſpeak,—may God be your friend.—I bid you adieu."

The ſon effectually diſcharged his duty to the remains of a kind and affectionate parent, and in every reſpect conducted himſelf with a degree of decorum ſuitable to the occaſion. After ſorrow had begun to abate its firſt gloom, in order to regain his former cheerfulneſs, he reſolved to give ſome of his acquaintances a call. A reſpectable family, of the name of Manlius, had the honour of his firſt viſit. Mr Manlius was a gentleman of a pleaſant manner, frank and facetious, with whom he had long lived on a very friendly and familiar footing. Having diſcourſed upon various topics, marriage at length became the ſubject of their converſation. Mr Griffin argued much in favour of a voluntary compact. He hinted. that arbitrary or compulſive meaſures might very well become the character of ſlaves ; but, in a free ſtate, was quite inconſiſtent with the independent ſpirit of virtue. He thought

M 2   freedom

freedom of choice fhould always be allowed, unlefs a ridiculous inclination made the connection
a matter of ridicule. In that cafe, he thought
it requifite, and confiftent with found policy, to
make ufe of every innocent ftratagem that could
tend to divert the progrefs of an affection that
prognofticated mifery in every view. He then end-
ed his harangue with a fhort comment on the beauty and good breeding of his friend's daughters.
To two of my girls, fays the father, I intend
giving a fortune; but as for the youngeft, I
mean to act contrary to the articles of your
creed; for whoever makes choice of her muft
pay me down eleven hundred pounds.

A demand fo fingular excited his curiofity.
He had been acquainted with her before, and
therefore required no great time to prove her
quality. He found her behaviour and good
fenfe, in every point, equal to her appearance.
The money he made no fcruple to pay; for he
plainly faw fhe was a jewel of ineftimable value.
After fettling thefe premifes with the father, he
went to acquaint the young lady with this extraordinary tranfaction. He modeftly intimated,
that he had made a purchafe of her; but told
her

her at the fame time, that, notwithstanding of
what had happened, he was refolved to take no
advantage of her inclination: And fo far from
infifting on the fulfilling of this engagement, or
laying the leaft reftraint upon her tafte, he in-
formed her, that from that moment fhe was at
liberty to chufe for herfelf. She politely thanked
him for his partiality; and added, that whatever
clouds might often concur to eclipfe the luftre of
fincere affection in fuch circumftances, on her
fide no remaining gloom darkened the profpect,
had any traces of exiftence, nor was the information in the leaft difagreeable to her. She
ftill further obferved, that fhe had but one heart
and one face, and thefe fhe would give him along
with her hand, without the leaft hefitation,
whenever he pleafed to make the demand.
Taking her at her word, the minifter was fent
for, and they were immediately made happy.
Her luftre, like the morning ftar, dazzled all
around. Her many virtues daily gained credit,
and increafed in beauty. But an unhappy accident drew the curtain of unexpected difafter,
over the fair profpect of their profperity, and

M 3   nipt

nipt haftily in the bud, all the flowers of their future joy.

A captain, of the name of *Dark-craft*, had anchored his fhip at no great diftance from this elegant dome, where virtue fat fmiling in every corner, and wore the garb of felicity every hour of the day. A wintry blaft unfortunately wafted him aboard. The captain and he began freely to tafte the juice of the vine. The jovial glafs went brifkly around; and as the liquor began to operate, it gave their tongues an additional volubility. Mr Griffin, as he might with great propriety, enlarged handfomely on the various endowments of his valuable partner. But the captain faid he fufpected much the extravagance of his eftimation; and to give plaufibility to his fuggeftion, he had recourfe to natural fimilitudes. The filver and drofs are not difcriminated, he obferved, till they undergo an experiment in the refiner's furnace; by the fame rule, virtue untried cannot claim the honour of being genuine. The other affured him, that he was perfectly convinced of his wife's fidelity; and would not hefitate a moment to pledge his eftate againft his fhip and cargo, that he would

find

find from any experiment he chofe to make, the reprefentation noway exaggerated. The captain took him at his word, and a legal bond was immediately written, and figned before witneffes, by both parties. Mr Griffin was to remain on board till the time agreed upon for the execution of the plot fhould expire, without giving the leaft inftruction to his wife, or divulging the fecret. The captain declared, he would cheerfully fulfil his part of the engagement, if in two days he did not accomplifh his point. Money, which is but too ready in every country to procure accomplices in the caufe of vice, was not without influence in this tranfaction. He foon found ways and means to gain the good opinion of Mrs Griffin's nurfe: *Sly-cut* was not very fqueamifh in her principles, being one of thofe creatures that would do any thing for pelf. She began her attack with grofs equivocation, made her believe that one of her friends had found a cheft with blankets on the fhore, and alledged, that it could not in the leaft feem a matter of furprife, that, in cafe of a fearch, fhe thought it would be perfectly fecure, with a character of her confequence; and declared, that fhe would

efteem

efteem the indulgence a particular favour, if fhe
would fuffer it to remain in her bed-room for
one night. Sufpecting no colour of treachery,
this amiable character at once gave her confent
to the propofal; and, under the darknefs of
night, this neft of mifchief was conveyed to her
apartment. A hole was made oppofite to his
eye, where he might take his obfervations; and
an infide lock, that he could open at pleafure,
gave him every neceffary fecurity.

At the proper hour of reft, this virtuous
beauty kneeled before her God, to exprefs her
gratitude, and implore the continuation of his
mercy. After having finifhed her devotion, fhe
began to undrefs; and this monfter of iniquity
was all attention. The vifible mark of a key
on her breaft, which was a figure very uncommon, furprifed him lefs than her bright appearance, and compofed manner. Before fhe lay
down, he faw her take a purfe from her pocket,
and put it into a cheft of drawers; a prize which
this demon of mifchief looked upon as already
in his clutches. So foon as he found this pa-
tronefs of virtue fafely afhore on the land of
reft, he ftole from his deteftable cabin, to look

for

for plunder,: He fearched the drawers, and foon
fecured whatever he found anfwerable to his
purpofe ; but when her profile and purfe fell
into his unhallowed hands, he quietly retired to
his lurking place, having enough for his purpofe
in poffeffion. At the dawn of day, the cheft
was removed, and this ravenous wolf once more
fet at liberty. Exulting in his wickednefs, he
haftened aboard, and boafted of favours he could
never have obtained : declared he had made
great progrefs in the fcience of aftronomy, and
expected he would admit his practice of aftrolo-
gy, from the fhape of the key on his wife's
breaft. He appealed to himfelf, if that difcovery
was not a fufficient proof, that he ftood fecure in
her favour. The other objected to it as a piece
of information he might eafily acquire, without
the leaft acquaintance with her. Producing her
profile and purfe, I hope then this will convince
you of my conqueft ; as being *argumentam ad
feminam ;* and added, that fhe was much pleafed
with his company, and wifhed him to repeat
his vifits as often as he could make it convenient. The poor infatuated hufband could not
refift the evidence, but fwallowed this doctrine
without

without the fmalleft doubt. He acted no part
of the prudent, honeft, and ingenuous hufband:
for, without mentioning the matter to his wife,
or giving her the leaft hint of his fufpicion, like
a poor filly fool, he delivers his charter to the
captain, and into the truth of his report made
no further inquiry. He applied to this raga-
muffin for fome of his hands, who got ready at
command, when the bufinefs was clearly underftood; for he was fhaking with fear, left by
fome accident his villany fhould be difcovered.
Having made all things fnug, Mrs Griffin's
confent was foon obtained, to accompany them
to what fhe thought a party of pleafure; but it
was a cruel ftratagem that haftened her fteps
into complicated mifery. They made away
with her from the land, and reaching a barren
rock at fome diftance from fhore, left her alone,
to make her complaint to the wilds and waves.
Her tears and entreaties were entirely fruitlefs,
and had no effect on the inhuman favages, to
whom her landing was intrufted. She was
fcarcely an hour in this unpleafant fituation,
however, when fhe faw a fhip in full fail,
coming near to the place where fhe was; and
kind

kind Providence, which often works miracles in
critical moments, foon appeared to alleviate her
calamity, and to convert her darknefs into light.
A hoop, which the rolling wave, in compaffion
for her diftrefs, drove within her reach, was
employed, with her handkerchief at one end of
it, as a fignal of diftrefs; and her little flag was
foon obferved. The captain, whofe name was
Titus Fairline, was by no means deftitute of
virtue or humanity, and therefore fent his boat
and hands immediately to her relief; and bore
clofe to the wind, till fhe was fafely brought
aboard. The honeft tars, without the leaft colour of charity, (as the account fhe gave of herfelf was not altogether fatisfactory), concluded,
that fhe was only a fafhionable woman of the
town, who having committed fome *faux paux*,
had been left upon that account, and not for the
building of a church. As foon as her tears had
ceafed to flow, the captain, who fuppofed them
to have proceeded from the danger fhe was in,
rather than from a fenfe of injured innocence, or
any delicacy of fentiment fhe might poffefs,
began to make propofals, quite too indelicate
for the modeft ear of his female paffenger.
                                          She

She feemed to bear them with fome degree of
patience, till he forgot that decency of language,
and that meafure of refpect, which virtue, confcious of its dignity, naturally expects; but then
fhe thought it perfectly requifite to affume a little
courage, and addrefs him with becoming firmnefs. " Sir, you feem to be very well verfed in
the rudiments of raillery; but fuch language as
yours, like wild birds notes, can never be
brought to any regular mufic. Theoginis the
poet obferves, that it is a great burden to a
lover of prattle to hold his tongue; but to fpeak
without the leaft fhadow of wit or common fenfe,
muft be equally burdenfome to his company.
Obfcene language is a breach of politenefs,
fhocks reafon, and deftroys morality. It is true,
the fituation in which you found me might give
countenance to various conjectures. To figures
any way uncommon, either in the heavens, or
on the earth, people are ready to annex what
meaning they pleafe. Human actions, which
admit of the leaft fufpicion, are often blackened
with an erroneous conftruction, and the colours
given them by him who attempts to unravel
their myfterious parts, fhew lefs or more of his

own

own difpofition. I am truly fenfible that, as my deliverer, I owe you many obligations. But if you fuppofe or expect that I am to repay this act of humanity at the expence of my honour and virtue; you will find yourfelf much miftaken. I fhall not hefitate one moment to execute the part of Lucretia, if you perfift in meafures fo deftructive to the peace of my mind. It is true, I am in your power; but if you offer to abufe that power, you muft anfwer at the bar of God, for fuch a complication of cruelties. Be not fur-prifed at the boldnefs of my language : for feve-rity, at times, is abfolutely neceffary, to guard honeft women from irreparable injury ; not only as you ufe your lead to guard you againft falfe foundings, but as veneration doth facred things, which often deters the moft daring of men from treating fteady virtue with infolence.

To the flaves of vice, contemplations of ge-nuine refinement are feldom familiar. All thofe figures which are written out in the language of folly, or which immorality records in the mind, tend to produce cloudy reflections ; and the premiums they beftow, are only the blufhes

of

of fhame. Suffer me further to repeat the words of a great poet and a Chriftian:

" Afpiring youth,
Strive to refift the fyren voice of vice,
Let none of her inchantments draw thee on
To guileful fhores, nor meads of fatal joy.
When wifdom proftrate lies, the foolifh foul
Is wrapt in vifions of unreal blifs;
And fading fame diffolves in air away:
Then 'tis too late to feize the prize of virtue."

The captain, finding a different chara&ter from what he expe&ted, immediately altered his tone; and began to treat her with all the politenefs of which he was mafter. From his mild and agreeable manner, fhe was made to believe, fhe had nothing further to fear from him: And he made fuch handfome apologies for his rude be-haviour, as were fufficient to convince her, that he was neither deftitute of found fenfe nor hu-manity. He told her, though his curiofity was fo much awakened, that it would have been more than an ordinary gratification, to have been favoured with her real hiftory, ftill he wifhed for no part of it which required a veil. And though he had no defire to purchafe infor-

I   mation

mation at the expence of creating pain to another; yet he would thank her for a candid reply
to one fingle queftion, viz. If ever fhe was
married, or if her hufband was in life? to
which fhe anfwered in the affirmative When
he underftood fhe had no money, he took the
opportunity, when fhe was upon deck, of writ-
ing a card, in which he inclofed twelve guineas,
wrapped it up in a pound of tea, and, when juft
going afhore, infifted fhe would accept of it,
and examine its contents when fhe was at leifure: which fhe accordingly did, and unexpectedly found herfelf miftrefs of a very great treafure. Her heart fwelled with joy and gratitude; and, in her prayers to Heaven, the happinefs of her generous benefactor was fincerely
remembered. She foon got herfelf neatly
equipped in a male drefs, which fhe fuppofed
would prove a greater fecurity to her than her
own. Having travelled fo far into the country,
that no report with regard to herfelf could
eafily overtake her, fhe began to inquire for a
mafter, and was foon received into the fervice
of Lord G——. Being poffeffed of the beft of
breeding, and exceedingly handfome, fhe was

foon

soon noticed, and of consequence brought to attend the table After she had been some time in the family, Lady G—— began to eye young Blyth-fame, which was the name she gave herself, as a much greater favourite than a servant. Having taken the advantage of Lord G——'s absence, she began with proposals which required categorical answers, and were fully as plain as they were pleasant. Blyth-fame, at first, acted as if the language had been unintelligible, and the signals displayed above her capacity to comprehend. There is a visible modesty or bashfulness, which commonly accompanies honest women: those who weigh their thoughts and manner in the scale of discretion, are easily known ; and by the reverse of the same proposition, the conduct of this Amarilles spoke a glaring deficiency in the laws of virtue and common prudence ; for she seemed to have held in contempt every colour of modesty. Blyth-fame, after conquering this gale of surprise, addressed her in a style as unexpected as it was seasonable : " The tenderness of Lord G—— to you, upon every occasion, merits a return the very reverse of your conduct to-day. Think

of

of him this moment as your hufband; think of him as he deferves; and I am perfuaded, you will blufh at the thought of acting a part fo un-generous, fo inconfiftent with the dignity which a character of your confequence ought to main-tain, and with the homage to which affection like his, is truly entitled. Without honour and mutual kindnefs, family-happinefs cannot rife to refpect, nor continue long to fubfift; and the fruit of thefe venerable virtues is as much efteemed by every honeft heart, as treachery, or yielding to every temptation, is deteftable and bafe. We are fure that it is not the fpinning, nor the quirking of a fyllogifm, that gives any weight to an argument, or any beauty to a cha-racter in the prefence of our God. No intereft is equal to that of fincerity, for gaining his ap-probation; and if we would preferve the affec-tion of thofe with whom we are any way fami-liar, the fame argument ftill holds good: for it is only by clofe application to the laws of virtue, and by mild generous offices, that we can hope for fuccefs. Therefore let me recommend to your perufal, the advice of Polonius in Hamlet,

"The

" The friend 'thou haft, and his adoption tried,
Grapple him to thy foul with hoops of fteel."

It is a great misfortune, when rank neglects
that Patrician fpirit of refinement, which is the
true, and ought to be the diftinguifhing ornament of dignity. For it is lamentable enough,
when birth, and a confpicuous ftation, look down
with a carelefs eye on moral beauties, or confider virtue and decency as a ceremony they
may eafily ftep over. Though pupils of this
degrading clafs have appeared in every age,
and will no doubt continue fo to do till the end
of the chapter, *that* does not in the leaft extenuate the folly, nor juftify the practice. And
every fenfible perfon will readily allow, that
the lefs fuch models are copied, fo much the
better. It is furely a delightful profpect to fee
emulation prevail among all ranks, in venera-
ting the facred bond of affection, which unites
mankind in the various relations in which they
ftand to each other ; and thofe who revere every
link, calculated to maintain its ufefulnefs and
beauty unblemifhed, merit the regard of Heaven,
and the admiration of the world around them.

I

I might eafily multiply examples, from the annals of different nations, of characters whofe memory and virtuous actions, were defervedly extolled and immortalifed by the hiftorians of their age and country.

Suffer me to repeat an extraordinary report fent to the Emperor of China: " Agreeable to the order of your Majefty, for erecting monuments to the honour of women, who have been celebrated for their continency, filial piety, or purity of manners, the viceroy of Canton reports, that, in the town of Sinhvei, a beautiful young woman, named Leang, facrificed herfelf to fave her virtue. In the 15th year of our Emperor Canghi, fhe was dragged by pirates into their fhip; and having no other way to efcape their barbarity, fhe threw herfelf headlong into the fea, being impelled by a momentary impulfe of preferring honour and virtue to life itfelf. We purpofe, according to your Majefty's order, to erect a triumphal arch for that young woman, and to engrave her ftory upon it, that it may be preferved in perpetual remembrance." I now conclude this plain honeft exhortation, by no other apology, than

affuring

affuring you, that, if you have judgement
enough to keep your own fecret, I fhall never
be the trumpeter of your folly ; providing you
give me no further trouble upon this fcore."
Notwithftanding of this friendly counfel, Lord
G—— no fooner reached home, than Blyth-
fame had her character blackened by the fouleft
afperfions. Colours of depravity were eafily
borrowed from an over-heated imagination, to
make her name and drefs appear perfectly awk-
ward. The nobleman, quite enraged, thought
even hanging too lenient a punifhment. She
was foon lodged in a gloomy apartment, that
perhaps never had the honour of fuch a gueft.
The refult of her trial was *banifhment for life.*
She wrote a letter with her own hand to Lord
G——, pleaded genteelly for a perfonal inter-
view, infifted much that he would condefcend
to vifit her, with two trufty witneffes ; and engaged to produce fuch proofs of innocence, as he
himfelf would readily admit. The folicitation
was penned with fuch effectual arguments, as
would have moved humanity lefs genuine than
Lord G——'s.

As foon as he appeared before her, fhe told
him,

him, that nothing but the utmoſt neceſſity could ever have induced her to make a diſcovery which could not fail to wound the feelings of one whom ſhe truly eſteemed; and, to be ſhort, gave him to underſtand, that his own happineſs could not but be greatly impaired, from the in-formation ſhe had to communicate. She then, with undiſſembled modeſty, diſcovered her breaſt; and added, that ſhe was an unfortunate female, doomed to fall under the imputation of crimes ſhe neither did, nor ever would wiſh to commit. Her language was now powerful enough to give her relation that colour of veracity, which but a few days before it could not command. Lord G——— admired her much, and went even ſo far as to make honourable propoſals;— but when he found ſhe could not accept of his offer, he without delay paid her three hundred pounds, for the unmerited injury her character had ſuf-fered. She then made haſte to leave a place ſo hoſtile to her reputation, and where many ſtrange reports were blazed abroad, with incredible rapi-dity. She poſted ſome days, without meeting a ſingle adventure, worthy of notice. Overtaking at laſt, upon the road, one of thoſe who perform

the

the office of a folicitor in courts of equity, fhe
engages him to inftruct her in the effentials of
his profeffion. She made fuch rapid progrefs in
the ftudy of law, that fhe was foon every where
admired; having all the graces that Chefterfield
gives to Marlborough, without the leaft title to
the oppofite charge, of being eminently illiterate.

As foon as fhe took up bufinefs for herfelf, in
the line of an Attorney, an amazing fuccefs pur-
fued her, and fame attended her banner where-
ever fhe appeared. Preffing bufinefs foon called
her to a diftant part of the country. When fhe
had reached the place of her deftination, fhe
found, in the houfe where fhe lodged, a poor
man, who had been in fome menial office about
the family, feized with a fevere colic, and
thought at the point of death. Blyth-fame,
whofe humanity had fuffered no diminution
from her good fortune, was exceedingly attentive
to him, and adminiftered cordials that gave im-
mediate relief. But how great was her pleafure and furprife, when fhe got a full view of
her patient, and read Theophilo Griffin in
every feature of his face. She afked, if ever he
had a female friend? He replied, that he had,

and

and that her name was Agnes Manlius. She then propofed to engage him for her fervant; but at the fame time, gave him to underftand, that fhe would only employ a faithful attentive perfon, and a man of character. He told her fhe might depend upon his honefty. Well, faid fhe, that is with me the principal requifite, and an apology for a variety of foibles. She then inquired into the character of the family; of which he gave her this candid defcription: Mr and Mrs True-faith disfigure not their creed; for it is not on particular days, nor yet for particular purpofes, that they ufe the articles of their religion: no, they are in reality what they profefs to be, plain, honeft, and induftrious characters, free from all guile and deceit.

But it will be neceffary, before I proceed further in the bufinefs, continued fhe, to know the fentiments of your mafter and miftrefs. This point was fpeedily fettled; for the matter was no fooner underftood, than their confent was freely obtained. She then and there met with a variety of pleafant incidents, and, among others, found Captain Fairline, in the perfon of her client: a difcovery which tended to intereft her

feelings,

feelings, and ftrengthen her exertions in his caufe. His owners were attempting to defraud him of a thoufand pounds, and had hired all the pettifoggers of that place againft him; when he was advifed to write for Blyth-fame, whofe reputation was current every where. Blyth-fame had all the technical terms of the law fo pat, that fhe foon confounded her opponents, and gained the plea, with expences. The honeft captain was much taken with the abilities of his lawyer, and told him to make his own terms. Captain Fairline, faid fhe, the generofity and goodnefs of your heart I well know; and as there is none prefent but ourfelves, to convince you that I have not the leaft doubt of your honour, allow me to inform you, that I am the very female you took from the rock, and for whom you inclofed the twelve guineas in a pound of tea. You muft promife me inviolable fecre-fy; and this is all the fee I demand. A gold watch, and a diamond ring, he would infift upon her accepting as a prefent: and then they parted in admiration of each other. She and her fervant went home, with an intention to fettle all her bufinefs, and return to her native country.

country. At leifure hours, fhe diverted herfelf
very much with Theophilo, and appeared upon
a more familiar footing with him,—than he had
any title to expect. She came home one day in
great glee, and told him, fhe had got flattering
news for him, which were worth a whole hand-
ful of money. She faid, fhe had been looking
out a wife for him, and had pitched upon a very
handfome girl, with whom, fhe was perfuaded,
he would live quite happy. The poor man
could only anfwer her at firft with tears; but
at laft he exclaimed, Alas! alas! all my happinefs of that kind is already decided. You feem,
continued fhe, to take the matter fo ferioufly,
that your complaint muft furely arife from fome
extraordinary caufe. To you, Mr Blyth-fame,
I fhould open my breaft without referve; and
from the familiarity with which you have treated me, fuch confidence you might very naturally
expect: for fince the firft day of my engagement
with you, the fcene of my life is not more
changed, than the difpofition of my mind: my
enjoyments are pregnant with inexpreffible tran-
quility. I have truly experienced more unin-
terrupted pleafure in one hour, than I had tafted

O   for

for feveral years. But, after all, I know, that,
for the crime I have committed, you will think
I ought to be difcharged from your fervice, as a
wretch unworthy of compaffion; while, at the
fame time, your goodnefs of heart will incline
you to pity my misfortunes. To complain of
difafters on fome particular occafions, faid his
mafter, is quite allowable; but to bear adverfity
with fortitude and filent refignation, is manly:
nay, it is more than manly, for it raifes human
nature above mortality. Think of the animating
fentiments of him who divinely exclaimed,

"Were I as tall as reach the fky,
Or grafp the ocean in a fpan,
I would be meafur'd by my foul;
The mind's the ftandard of the man."

Or, in other words, "My hand I faften on the
ftars, and bid earth roll, nor feel her idle whirl,"
You may thoughtlefsly fuppofe, the complexion
of your troubles fo dark and unufual, that others
cannot feel the emotion of kindred fympathy,
nor a compaffionate wifh to fhare in your cares;
but fuch a fuppofition is rafh and ungenerous,
and therefore ought not to be indulged. Faith
recommends

recommends to our attention, the model of all
refinement. If he who is a stranger to imper-
fection, bears with the best of us, we should
frequently reflect on his mildness and patience;
and endeavour, as much as possible, to imitate
and exemplify the same disposition to our fel-
low-sufferers. Sorrows are made light by sharing them; and perhaps your crime may not appear to me in the same dark colours, with
which the painting of a gloomy imagination,
which is ever apt to exaggerate the leading linea-
ments of the picture, may represent it to yourself. To feed continually on melancholy or
cloudy images, is quite unsuitable to the dignity
of a Christian; neither is it paying proper respect to the Author of our mercies, who giveth
us all things liberally to enjoy, and upbraideth
not. Industry is neither calculated to create
pain, nor to sow the seed of affliction, (which
is a plant of spontaneous growth), but the balm
which religion kindly imparts to the dejected
spirit; and if it cannot completely heal the
wound, it will at least abate its pain, by engaging the body in some useful exercise, or the
mind in some suitable train of thought. Al-

though

though the child may be out of temper with the
parent, for refufing at certain times the gratification of his fancy; yet he may be made fenfible,
at a future period, how much the judgement of
the father was preferable to his own; and of
the gratitude he owes him for the intereft he
took in his happinefs. Unexpected treafures
may fall into the hand of a mifer, and princes
may confer public honours on whom they pleafe;
but the inheritance of a virtuous name, and the
veneration of ages, are badges of diftinction
which muft in fome meafure be the fruit of
our own exertions, rather than of accidental circumftances. The man that would be truly rich,
fays Seneca, muft not fo much increafe his fortune, as ftudy to retrench his luxury. Therefore, in place of nurfing a fpirit of difcontent,
how much more commendable is it, whatever
our fituation may be, to practife the leffons of
Chriftian philofophy. Should we only take the
trouble to compare notes with many around us
in the world, in all probability, we might often
fee caufe not to repine, but rather to be thank-
ful for our own fituation. It is a command of
temper that conftitutes the character of all heroes;

roes; and it is a great comfort, as well as an object worthy of particular attention, that if we are not wholly exempted from sufferings, our conduct under them should be such, as to declare that we wish to remove the cause of their continuation. I hope you are now fully persuaded, that I am inclined rather to mitigate your present complaint, than to create you new distresses; and therefore I expect you will favour me with a free and candid relation of a disappointment that seems to have been attended with particular incidents.

He then began, and gave her a minute detail of the whole business between himself and *Dark-craft*. The treachery of the nurse rose to her view in all its deformity; and she felt in her bosom a glow of displeasure, which required all her discretion to conceal. However, she called to her aid all the philosophy of which she was mistress; and assuming, as much as she was able, the air of a disinterested person, made use of some tender expressions, in a condoling strain, assured him of the continuation of her esteem and patronage; and added, that his integrity, she thought, deserved a much better fate than that

O 3   of

of the cruel injury he had met with. "But Theophilo, "said she," your wife may be still alive."
His reply gave a negative to the suppofition :
" What would you fay, if that odious fellow
had impofed upon your credulity, and found
ways and means to fteal the articles he produced to you, as a proof of your wife's incon-
tinency. If you was convinced of this, how
would you treat him?" I would pray God to
give him a fight of his wickednefs, and think
he had acted a bafe part indeed. " The refinement
of your mind, I cannot help admiring ; for furely that generous benevolent fpirit, that tramples
down revenge, that triumphs over premeditated
villany, or filences the clamour of its enemies,
is entitled to efteem, though bewildered by rafh
credulity. I muft own, that I feel myfelf much
interefted in your caufe ; and as I intend foon to
vifit that part of the world, I will ufe every exertion to recover your eftate." Theophilo had no
great inclination to appear in a place where his
misfortunes had been fo complicated and uncommon ; but Blyth-fame infifted upon his going, and
in his prefent character of a fervant. When
they reached her father's houfe, the whole family

mily attacked the bafe man, as they called him, and threatened to make an end of him, without either judge or jury.' Upon your peril, touch him even with one of your fingers, faid fhe, he is my fervant, and if he has committed any action out of character, juftice is open, and the law of the land muft either acquit or condemn him. A warrant to apprehend him was immediately obtained. Blyth-fame attended him to his place of confinement; and when fhe took her leave, recommended refignation and a good heart; for that fhe would fee him foon, and fafely fet at liberty. She thought it was perfectly requifite to fecure *Dark-craft;* and went herfelf with the party to execute the warrant. She furprifed him over a jovial bowl, with his frothy companions; told him, that his villany was fully detected, and vengeance ready to take hold of him. The keys and the charter were immediately fecured; and when fhe came to the apartment where her own nurfe lay fick, fhe could fcarcely reftrain her indignation. "You wicked woman," fhe exclaimed, " you are a difgrace to your fex: what could have tempted you to treat your fofter child with fuch unmerited barbarity?

You

You are in a few days to appear before God, the righteous judge of all, whom you have egregioully offended: I pray that he may have mercy upon your foul, and meet you with a different treatment from what you gave her." She made a candid confeffion of her guilt; and the taking down of her depofition did not in the leaft leffen her horror: confufion and terror every moment ftared her in the face, and in the greateft agony fhe foon expired. Againft *Dark-craft*, the proof was fo clear, that he could not efcape: He was fentenced to be hanged. The judges and lawyers were quite aftonifhed at the eloquence and addrefs of Blyth-fame; but, notwithftanding of this, the firft day of Griffin's trial, produced no great caufe of exultation. After the Court was difmiffed, Blyth-fame made up to Mr Manlius, praifed his horfe very much, and afked what might be his value? Thirty guineas, he replied. She immediately paid the money; and as foon as fhe had deliverance, fhe took a piftol out of her pocket, and fhot the horfe dead upon the fpot. Mr Manlius feemed to be out of temper at this mad action, as he called it. Blyth-fame told him, fhe would

foon

foon make a public reply to his obfervation.
Againft next court-day, fhe begged the judges
attention to a particular circumftance; then related the altercation between herfelf and Mr
Manlius; and afked, if they thought her conduct
any way culpable, or deferving of punifhment?
The prevailing voice declared in her favour.
Well, faid fhe, by the fame rule of reafoning,
this man muft come off clear. I underftand he
has paid ten or eleven hundred pounds for his
wife; and if he had fhot her as I did my horfe,
who could blame him? I fhould think the man
that fold her ought to be the very laft perfon
that fhould open his lips upon the fubject.
The matter had been fo nicely ftated, that neither judges nor jury had any fcruple to acquit
him. She then made a full difcovery of herfelf,
in open court. Theophilo, you have now by
the hand Agnes Manlius; after breaking afun-
der the clouds of falfe accufation, we are now
upon a level; for if once you made a purchafe
of me, I have now faved your life. She then
looked to the judges, and expreffed a wifh, not
to take poffeffion of her eftate, with her hands
imbrued in the blood of *Dark-craft*. She then
pleaded

pleaded for a mitigation of his fentence; which was accordingly changed into perpetual banifh-ment.

I fhall now leave Mr and Mrs Griffin in the country where I found them, and allow them the quiet enjoyment of their own eftate, with a conftant flow of invariable happinefs: for I truly think they deferve no lefs. And as I mentioned in the beginning, that the defcription is moftly indebted to the colours of imagination, and not built upon facts; I fuppofe this apology will be deemed fufficient for the liberty I have taken, and free me from the charge of intended impofition.

The moral it inculcates is quite plain: Though God, in his wife Providence, and for ends beft known to himfelf, allows lawlefs proceedings to rage, and fometimes to prevail in the world; though virtue has frequently felt the infults of triumphant vice, and for a while been bafely trampled under foot; we fee it often, by unac-countable windings, re-afcending from obfcurity, and coming mildly forward to view; while the wickednefs of the wicked iffues in a fpeedy or difgraceful end.

We

[167]

We fee the fibres of many falfe plots won-
derfully traced through the dark fteps of artful
contrivance, or fecret machinations; and their
deformity expofed to the glare of day.

The favour of God is always interefted in the
caufe of virtue: even when ftruggling with the
clouds of unmerited reproach, a confcioufnefs of
rectitude helps much to difarm the fting of
trial; and what ought to make the purfuit of
virtue an object of emulation is, that her votaries are, or fhould be, adorned with trophies of
unfading fame.

Where true affection takes a feat in the foul,
and fincerity fecures the key of the heart, fuch
progrefs will foon be manifeft, that the face of
the object we love will feem to upbraid us, if
ever we entertain an improper idea; and criminal defires will labour in vain to meet with indulgence. The paffions of the human breaft
are many, and no lefs various in their nature
than the colours by which they are delineated.
Artifice, under borrowed features, may ftretch
its hand to grafp the prize that is not its due:
But the mafk, however artfully decorated, is too
thin and coarfe to fcreen long from detection

the

the deformity it would attempt to hide. And whenever we fee wicked defigners furprifed in their own fnare, expofed in their own drefs, and difappointed of their fecret and infamous intentions,—we rejoice in fuch difcoveries, feel fincere pleafure at the efcape of innocence, and blefs that propitious power, who wifely overrules the affairs of the world. To all fingular cafes we attend with a fort of enthufiafm; at the relation of intricate and interefting fcenes which touch the heart, the breaft glows with anxious emotions. When we fee juftice impartially adminiftered, integrity fnatched from imminent danger, and virtue meet with its deferved reward,— we find a gratification which yields us more than ordinary pleafure. In the firft book of Kings, ch. iii. 19. we fee a plain inftance of treachery completely detected. With aftonifhment we behold the piercing judgement, and quick fancy, of the wife King of Ifrael. Unbiafed integrity, connected with tender movements of humanity, are amiable qualifications in any character; but much more fo in perfons of eminence: not that fuch examples are rare, but becaufe from diftinguifhed perfonages they have

always

always a commanding influence. Two women
appeared before him, claiming the living child :
the King interested himself keenly in this business,
and his ingenuity in finding out the real mother
may well be called an acute stroke of a happy invention: "He called for a sword, and said, Divide
the living child, and let each have an half :
then spake the mother, for her compassion was
kindled towards her son, O my Lord, give her
the living child, and slay him not." These
words are richly coloured with the tender feelings of a generous heart. What an affecting
scene ! the agitation of her mind, how difficult
to describe ! When she saw the stern hand of
death darkly stretched forth, to tear the babe of
her bosom, from sharing in her future joy,—
anxiety must have filled up every painful period
which elapsed, and serious suspence stood trem-
bling for the final decision. The superior quality of tender feelings, like the bright beams of
the sun, is expressively displayed, not only by
the radiance of its own power, but by a contrast
with the callous colours of insensibility. Rude
tracts, and uncultivated mountains, make the
beauty of the fertile plain more attractive ; we

P   could

could not form an adequate idea of the rich materials that compofed the mind of the mother,
had not this unfeeling character of an impoftor
appeared. What an odious picture does the
whole of her conduct exhibit! all that feemed
to give her any concern, was the cenfure of the
world; for as to any remains of virtue, or virtuous principles, thefe are altogether out of the
queftion. I blufh for her barbarity, " let the
child be neither thine nor mine but divide it."

What a bafe heart is here brought to view!
who can repeat the expreffion without feelings
of difapprobation? the language and tone of indignation are naturally annexed to fuch a character. Where no remains of benevolence or
modefty poffefs the heart, it is quite impoffible
that fuch a barren foil can produce any of the
fruits of piety, or refpect to God.

Humanity and cruelty are fo widely different
in their nature, that to fuppofe a coalition to
take place between them, would be no lefs than
a contradiction in terms. The pretended mother,
while fhe continued under the fcreen of night,
thought herfelf perfectly fecure from the blaft of
ridicule. The deceitful glofs which covered the

mean

mean furniture of her grovelling foul, was all
the effect of malice, or the fpume of envy; for
the deftruction of the child, to her, was a matter of moonfhine, while the anxiety it would
produce in the breaft of the mother would oc-
cafion a cloud of forrow, and an age of pain.
But from a ftate of painful fufpence, her mind
was transformed to unexpected tranquillity, by
the impartial fentence which was fuddenly pro-
nounced: " Then faid the King, Give her the
living child, and flay him not; for this is his
mother." The mind that is inured to the paths
of virtue, always carries with it the fureft anti-
dote againft the venom of reproach, and eyery
thing elfe by which vice attempts to ftigmatize
it. It is not only neceffary that wickednefs be
denied applaufe, but that goodnefs be commend-
ed in proportion to its quality : for it would be
a pity to fuffer the garland of virtue and religion to remain, or to fade, on the brow of a
falfe pretender.

The fenfible female will require no reafoning
to convince her, that the beginning of ill-habits
is no lefs to be dreaded than their conclufion ;
and therefore will never join in the laugh of

thofe who affect to be witty, at the expence of humanity, virtue, or religion. She will fhew no fhynefs in acquainting them, that fuch fub-jects are quite difagreeable to her tafte; that fhe is neither out of conceit with virtue, nor yet ready to embrace vice. It was an ufual, but political charge, given of old, to fight neither great nor fmall; but only the King of Ifrael. So thefe Bolinbrokes, Voltaires, Roffeaus, Gib-bons, and the modern Deift Paine, who have openly declared themfelves the enemies of man-kind, having ftudied the fhorteft way to anarchy, take every opportunity of making favage thrufts at religion, and of wickedly expofing it as the butt of their ridicule; juft as if merit confifted in deftroying what is facred, and ferioufly in-terefting to every civilized nation. A profane wit is indeed a contemptible character: in the time of the Pfalmift, the *fool* thought the very fame things that thefe do. And to deferve the epithet *fool* can be no great compliment. Their prohibited artifices are much worfe than of no value, and therefore fhould meet with no favour. The learned Bifhop Watfon, whofe character, as a man of letters, is defervedly

eftablifhed,

eſtabliſhed, and whoſe piety and goodneſs of heart are entitled to laſting reſpect, has, with his uſual ingenuity, painted infidels in the deformed colours due to their character; and ſo much to the purpoſe, as one would think ſufficient to make all thoſe in the leaſt tinctured with their principles, bluſh, repent, and attempt reformation, when they take a ſerious view of the pitiful picture which their own character exhibits.

Mr Erſkine, our Ciceronian Orator, that moving library of knowledge and information, never fails, in his public exhibitions, whenever an apt opportunity occurs, to pay this claſs well home; and his reaſoning is ſo clear, his wit ſo genuine, and his ſatire ſo keen, that the wounds he inflicts muſt be ſeverely felt.

A reſpectable character, with whom I have the honour to be acquainted, and whoſe converſation I have often thought a perfect luxury, in talking one day of Deiſtical writers, made this ſenſible remark, " Men's words are ſoon forgotten, but the performances of thoſe who write for the edification of mankind exiſt for ages: when ſcepticiſm ſpeaks with audacity,

P 3   and

and infidelity is feen without a mafk, the confequence is melancholy, and much more dangerous than many are aware of. If fome will be
fingular, and are difpofed to entertain diftempered and noxious opinions, it would be fomewhat honeft to bury their fentiments in their
own breafts, and not to wound the feelings of
others, by a bold avowal of them." This
frenzy of deftroying the finews of virtue, or the
happinefs of mankind, was long lefs known than
it has been of late years; becaufe it fo glaringly
depreciated the dignity of human nature, that it
was allowed to lurk in the den of darknefs,
where it fhould always be confined. I fhall
now take my leave of it, by wifhing its deluded
votaries a more generous way of thinking.

In the early ages of the world, we find meafures for encouraging virtue publicly eftablifhed in many countries. The Egyptians, I
think, had once a law which ordained, that
the character and actions of thofe eminently
diftinguifhed for moral refinement fhould be
folemnly canvaffed before their beft judges, in
order to regulate what degree of fame was due
to their memory. No dignity however exalted,

no

no abilities however extraordinary, could un-
juftly feize, in the competition, the prize of genuine virtue. Moral refinement alone was the
road to honour, and the character by which
their names were eternifed and raifed to facred
refpect. To ingenuous minds this was a powerful incentive to the purfuit of virtue, and alfo
a ftrong reftraint to the wicked and thoughtlefs,
in the career of vice. Greece had many examples to boaft of, and the Romans were always liberal in their encomiums and rewards,
when female merit reached the pinnacle of approbation. If the diftaff of Tanaquil, the con-
fort of Tarquin, was thought worthy of notice
in their public records, and confecrated to the
temple of Hercules, as a memorial of acknowledged induftry, and a copy worthy of imitation,—with the fame propriety, the Renfrewfhire
jeffamine may be thought a diftinguifhed copy
of virtue and conjugal affection. What a generous exclamation ! " My cloaths, and whatever
elfe you chufe, are before you ; but, for God's
fake, fave my hufband's life !" What feeling
heart could behold her on her bended knees,

and

and hear her tender requeſt without ſympathy and admiration!

For the encouragement of virtue, and the reward of merit, it were to be wiſhed ſubordination would take place in the female world, as well as in the ſcenes of civil life. Warriors who ſignalize themſelves in the ſervice of their country, are raiſed to lucrative ſtations, and the rank of nobility. Penſions alſo are given to men eminent for their abilities; while an amiable accompliſhed female, whoſe bright example is of ſuch ſingular intereſt to the ſociety with which ſhe is connected, is not much noticed, excepting by a few of her intimate acquaintances; and, when ſhe is no more, her good actions vaniſh with herſelf. The *bona dea* was a diſtinction inſtituted at Rome, and might have continued with fame unſullied, had it not been for the abuſe it met with from a baſe character.

It were to be wiſhed our amiable Queen, who is an example of ſingular refinement to all her ſubjects, would invent ſome honorary title, or diſtinguiſh ſome of our deſerving females with badges of dignity, correſponding to the character they maintained, and the part they acted, as an

incitement

incitement to virtue, and the study of mental improvement.

So much for the Mental Pick; and if I have made use of any unguarded or indelicate thought, calculated in the least to hurt the morals, or wound the feelings of the reader, I hope they will have charity enough to ascribe it to inadvertency, rather than to a voluntary bias towards immorality : for if I have penned any indecent expression, I may honestly say, it was more than I either wished or intended.

A false mirror, which misreprefents its object, or alluring artifices which fear the light, and lead to the precipice of ruin, or help to lull the mind asleep in the lap of profaneness, vanity, or self-sufficiency, I have considered as rude invaders of the happiness of an accomplished female. And, from principle as well as from taste, I have had a sincere desire to keep at a distance, if possible, from forming an acquaintance with such hostile imposters. Flattery, the avowed enemy of improvement, which too often serves as fuel to feed the flames of levity, I have had no inclination to enter into terms of reconciliation with, nor to join in the excursion of its consumptive

party.

party. But how far I have kept clofely to fuch
refolutions, others will be more competent
judges of than myfelf. Amidft the many elegant and learned productions, with which our
age and country abound, that my fimple Pick
fhould meet with favour or indulgence, at the
expences of folding together the inftructive and
entertaining pages of approved performances,
that merit the moft ferious and attentive perufal,
is more than I can reafonably expect; and
therefore I fhall banifh fuch flattering thoughts :
for it makes its appearance more by way of a
memorial of hints, than a fyftem of inftruction.
At an idle hour, or a folitary walk, it might
help, plain and artlefs as it is, to fuggeft ideas
productive either of amufement or improvement.
That the female of character and merit may
every where meet with the refpect due to mental beauties, will never be an eye-fore to me.
Though I have not the ingenuity of Ariftogenes,
nor can furprife Clementina with her own exact
refemblance, as he did Celonia with his handfome looking-glafs; yet fhe may obferve, from
this faint attempt of a weak artift, what he

would

would be willing to perform, if his abilities were equal to his inclination. ·

I ſhall have no objeƈtions that the plains of her reſidence ſhould be richly perfumed with the fragrance of every amiable accompliſhment. May not only the virtues of the new name mentioned in ſcripture, known to thoſe only who receive the heavenly appellation, be liberally imparted to her, but may her happineſs be alſo made ſtationary.

If the external conſtruƈtion of her frame is neat and comely, may the internal temper of her mind be equable and virtuous: May her frame be more laſting, and her beauty more durable, than the tranſient fragrance, or fading bloom. of a puny ſummer-flower: May it continue to flouriſh with eternal verdure, and be bright like the ſun in the height of his beauty. That the bleſſings of health and happineſs may ever ſmile around her, and the favour of her God, without an eclipſe, continue her inheritance in time and eternity, is the ſincere deſire of

PHILO GUNA.

CPSIA information can be obtained
at www.ICGtesting.com
Printed in the USA
BVOW06s1930090717
488900BV00005B/53/P